MEN
STEPPING FORWARD

Leading Your Organization on the Path to Inclusion

ELISABETH KELAN

BRISTOL
UNIVERSITY
PRESS

First published in Great Britain in 2023 by

Bristol University Press
University of Bristol
1–9 Old Park Hill
Bristol
BS2 8BB
UK
t: +44 (0)117 374 6645
e: bup-info@bristol.ac.uk

Details of international sales and distribution partners are available at
bristoluniversitypress.co.uk

© Bristol University Press 2023

British Library Cataloguing in Publication Data
A catalogue record for this book is available from the British Library

ISBN 978-1-5292-3002-4 paperback
ISBN 978-1-5292-3003-1 ePub
ISBN 978-1-5292-3004-8 ePdf

The right of Elisabeth Kelan to be identified as author of this work has been
asserted by her in accordance with the Copyright, Designs and Patents Act 1988.

Cover design: Hayes Design and Advertising
Front cover image: Silhouette feet © g.roman/Freepik
Bristol University Press use environmentally responsible
print partners.
Printed and bound in Great Britain by CPI Group (UK) Ltd,
Croydon, CR0 4YY

CONTENTS

ABOUT THE AUTHOR

Elisabeth Kelan is Professor of Leadership and Organization at Essex Business School, University of Essex. She holds a Leverhulme Trust Major Research Fellowship [MRF-2019–069] to study gender, inclusion and digitalization in the context of the future of work. She is an expert on men as change agents for gender equality, women in leadership, generations at work and diversity, inclusion and belonging.

PREFACE

"Why don't we find a woman to look after our gender equality agenda" was a sentence that I heard regularly when gender equality in organizations was discussed. The assumption was that to tackle gender equality women needed to lead on the subject. However, this has changed. In similar conversations, men in leadership positions now ask, "What can I do for gender equality?" Men are taking an active role in gender equality in the workplace and beyond. This book addresses how men can be change agents for gender equality in the workplace.

The book is based on research and advisory work on leadership for gender inclusion that I have engaged with for over one decade. But why study the subject in the first place? After having researched gender, diversity and inclusion in a variety of settings since being a student, I became increasingly gripped by how change in regard to gender equality can take shape. Yet, most research and interventions attempted to 'fix the women'. The focus was on developing women. While nothing is wrong with this as such,

I increasingly felt that cultures of organizations have to change to allow for inclusion to flourish. One of the standard responses I heard time and time again is that we need to involve leaders if we want to change organizations. That seemed logical to me but when I looked for research on that topic, there was not much there. In addition, it seemed obvious that the majority of those leaders are going to identify as men. Yet how men can be change agents for gender inclusion was not a topic that was researched well at that time. Luckily that has changed since then and a few more studies on men's leadership for gender inclusion have emerged but they are still situated at the margins of academic fields.

The book draws mainly on two of my own studies as well as related literature that might help to understand particular ways in which men can become more inclusive leaders. The first study is based on CEOs who were supportive of gender equality and had publicly lent their support to create gender equality in their organization. In other words, these CEOs were progressive in terms of gender relations and were supporting gender equality in their organizations. With most CEOs being men, the project was largely about what men can do for gender equality.

During the CEO project, one of the CEOs told me that his ability to create change in regard to gender equality in the workplace is rather limited. In other areas, he can bring about great change but with gender equality it is much more difficult. I asked him why that was the case and he responded that this is due the 'permafrost of middle management'. In his view, it was difficult if not impossible to melt the permafrost of middle management to allow middle managers to change their ways towards more gender-inclusive behaviours. Particularly men, who are the majority in middle management positions, were constructed as difficult to engage.

This inspired a second piece of research, which was guided by the question what men in middle management positions can do to create gender equality in the workplace. I knew that if I would interview middle managers they probably would struggle to detail the everyday activities that they engage in to support gender equality. I therefore decided that an approach that entails observation would be most suitable to find out what men in middle management positions can do to support gender equality. I worked with a range of organizations to identify middle managers who were perceived as doing gender inclusion well. This was not an easy endeavour because many organizations struggled to identify a man in a middle management position who they perceived as leading on gender equality. In a sense that shows the extent of the issue. Eventually, I identified men in middle management positions who walked the talk on gender equality. I job shadowed them to document and analyse how they support gender equality in the work context. This meant that I observed their daily activities. As part of this project I transformed some of the findings into comic strips. The comic strips were not intended to be funny as such. However, many people have since told me that they found them funny because they portray such everyday interactions of how gender inequality emerges.[1]

This book is written for men who are interested in becoming leaders for gender equality. Based on my research there are three attitudes of men towards gender equality. First, men might be actively resisting gender equality due to a variety of reasons often related to the fact that they themselves feel disadvantaged through a focus on gender equality. Second, there are men who are supportive of gender equality already. I have largely researched this group of men. Finally, there are those men in the middle. They want to get better at gender inclusion but do not really know how to do that. It is probably those men who are in this third middle category who can profit most from this book. However, even those who are already being gender-inclusive leaders might benefit from this book. For the first category of men, those resisting gender equality, I offer an alternative framing of how gender inclusion could be a career accelerator rather than a hindrance which is one of the most surprising findings from my research.[2]

The book is about how men can change gender relations in the workplace. While the focus is on the workplace, it is evident that many of the practices will intersect with private life. For instance, a man talking about picking up his children from school or being unavailable for a 7 am breakfast meeting can challenge gender perceptions in the workplace and is an important part of men's change agency even though it relates to a 'private' activity. Arrangements and responsibilities in the private life are central for how gender relationships are reproduced or challenged but the perspective taking in this book is one, which focuses on the workplace as the primary concern. This does not mean that men's leadership in the private sphere is not meaningful or important. Much the contrast. However, the vantage point of this book is paid employment and non-paid work is considered in regard to how it is perceived in the workplace.

The book uses 'men' as a shorthand to represent the majority group in many organizational settings. The research also applies to transgender men and people who identity as gender-diverse. Equally, many individuals who identify as women will also profit from this book. However, the focus of the book is on what majority men can do to become gender-inclusive leaders. These majority men of course also differ from one another: a younger man in the workplace will have different perspectives than an older man; a gay man will have different perspectives to a straight man; and a white man will have different perspectives to an Asian man. These differences among men are important and meaningful but for the purpose of this book, I will largely talk about being a man as the part of the identity that I am most concerned with.

The structure of the book follows the change-maker framework that I will outline in the Chapter 1. It contains three themes: visioning, enabling and modelling. Each of those themes are discussed in turn from a practical perspective. Chapter 5 of the book draws the different threads together to provide you with a course of action. If you are interested in the underlying research, you will find a list of published articles and reports in the acknowledgements and in the endnotes.

1
THE PATH OF THE CHANGE MAKER

" I could get my organization to paint all buildings orange tomorrow, but the organization will not budge on changing the culture towards more gender equality." Marcus, who was leading a major professional services firm, clearly showed his frustration that change towards more gender inclusion is difficult to achieve. I asked him why he was pursuing gender equality in the first place. It is clearly not an easy change. His response: "I want to leave a legacy." A legacy that outlives him when he is no longer in charge. Many other CEOs I interviewed echoed this sentiment. Leaving a legacy was a major driver for their engagement in gender equality. Of course leaving a legacy often did not relate only to gender equality. However, gender equality was selected as a way to leave a legacy exactly because it is hard to achieve. Many senior leaders talked about how their leadership can make a difference to achieve this difficult change and once achieved it would persist for a long time.

Change and leadership are intertwined. In this chapter, I will outline the model of the change maker for gender equality. Let's begin with the word 'leadership'. Etymologically the modern verb 'to lead' goes back to Old English and has its origin in Germanic; one of its meanings is to show the way or to follow the path.[1] We can imagine leadership as a path where we guide others and show the way. There is movement and transit entailed in this term, which already connotes that there is a change of location. This original concept of leadership as guiding others and changing location is central for how leadership is understood in this book. Gender-inclusive leadership is here seen as taking others with us on the path to gender equality.

This marks a departure from how leadership is often understood on a daily basis. If we think about a leader, we might think of a hierarchical position and being at the top of a hierarchy. We might want to find out what the traits, qualities and characteristics of those leaders are. For example, are these leaders charismatic or not? However, leadership is also understood as what people actually do – the mundane activities that unfold on a daily basis. Leaders are then not only those at the top of the organization but leadership can be expressed at any level of hierarchy. Of course the type of leadership a junior person can perform is different to that of a middle manager or a senior leader, but it is a form of leadership none the less. Even without much power and authority imbued by an organizational structure individuals can guide others to lead change.

If we see leadership as guiding others on a path, you need direction and you need a goal of where the path is going to lead. This is the intention, a shared goal or in other words the direction of travel. Core to leadership is that you cannot do leadership on your own. You need people who follow you. In a hierarchical structure you might have reward and punishment for achieving certain goals, but the traditional reward and punishment logic is more applicable to management than to leadership. Leadership is much more about inspiring others and influencing them to follow you, even if you do not have formal authority. People follow you because they believe that you can show them the path. How you influence them often happens through interactions. This means that, through everyday activities, you convince others to follow you on a path. These daily activities constitute leadership.

The path also entails the idea of movement and travel. This is the change that results from leadership. It is perhaps not surprising that many people who want to develop as leaders seek out change projects in an organization. Charlie, for instance, who is a middle manager in the pharmaceutical industry, wanted to develop his leadership capabilities to advance in the organization. From feedback, he learned that leading a change project, particularly one where he has to lead through influence rather than authority, would tick this box. Looking for a range of opportunities to lead a change project, he realized that the organization's efforts towards gender equality would be ideal. The change programme aligned with his values and would provide the change leadership capabilities that he was seeking.

Motherhood penalty and daddy bonus: women and men of the organization

Gender equality is high on the policy agenda in most organizations.[2] The need for change is commonly bolstered by citing some striking figures such as the small number of women in CEO positions (in case you are wondering, currently 5 per cent globally[3]). These small numbers are then used to argue that gender change has not been achieved yet and requires more action. Such a representation also focuses the attention on women in leadership. Adding more women to leadership is equated with achieving gender equality.

Another common topic is to address women's roles as mothers by focusing on initiatives that seek to address work-life integration or flexible working. Although these initiatives are presented as open to all, it is a focus on work-life integration that is expected to be particularly beneficial for working mothers. This was discussed particularly during the COVID-19 pandemic where during school closures mothers were said to shoulder the brunt of care work in the home.

These constructions are interesting from a number of angles. First, all women are seen as potential mothers.

The 'motherhood penalty' commonly refers to the wage difference where having children is linked to lower salary in mothers.[4] Not only do women who are mothers advance slower in their careers, it has been shown that all women regardless of whether they are mothers or not, are seen as potential mothers.[5] Moreover, the association of women and work-life integration means that men and fathers are often not part of the conversation. Some progressive companies have changed this recently by for instance running campaigns to support fathers taking care leave.

The glass ceiling describes the phenomenon that women have the top of the organization in sight yet cannot reach it. However, rather than just facing a glass ceiling, women are said to confront a labyrinth of leadership with many twists, turns, and dead ends.[6] To address this there is a plethora of initiatives that are designed to develop women as leaders, which range from women's leadership development programmes over coaching to making gender biases more visible. While all of these activities might be worthwhile, a more holistic and systematic perspective on gender in organizations is required. In many ways, gender in organizations can be considered as a profound change process that organizations embark on.

Although achieving gender equality is often framed as 'just another change process', that is not the case. Achieving gender equality is deeply connected to how society is structured. Most societies employ gender as a structuring device dividing people into women and men using a binary.[7] In most societies is the gender binary of male/female and masculine/ feminine structuring societies in a multitude of ways. This binary is also hierarchically organized, that is the male is valued over the female and the masculine is valued over the feminine. Furthermore, the male and masculine is often taken as the norm while female and feminine is the deviation of the norm. This traditional division of gender goes hand in hand with the different spheres that men and women are supposed to inhabit. Men are supposed to be in the public sphere such as politics and business and women are supposed to inhabit the private sphere of the home. This 'supposed to' is relevant because we all know of a multitude of examples where these expected gender roles are not matched with lived reality. We know men, often but not exclusively younger ones, who want to be involved fathers and not only take paternity leave but also work part-time. While those ideas about what men and women are supposed to do appear old-fashioned and misaligned with the experiences of women and men in many parts across the world, the gender division continues to exist and shape society. Failing to acknowledge this means that how change in regard to gender relations is conceptualized remains simplistic, trivial and uncomplicated. The gender binary is at the heart of why gender relations are difficult to change.

Many organizations aim to alter gender relations just like they would tackle other issues. Setting targets, measuring and taking mediating actions when things do not work out. While this might work with standard business problems, gender is not a standard business issue because it harks back to how societies are organized based on gendered lines. Putting a change programme for gender in place and expecting it to yield results in the next quarter, is highly unrealistic as the experiences of many organizations shows. Organizations have been trying to change gender for at least the last forty years. Surely the number of women in senior leadership positions has increased during that period but progress continues to be slow.

The reasons for the slow progress of change in spite of a myriad of initiatives is likely to the found in a simplistic understanding of gender. Most organizations focus on the obvious – increasing the number of women – without seriously considering how gender is embedded into the structures of the organization itself. How work is organized, how it is allocated and who gets credit for it is still heavily influenced by perceptions of gender. The most enlightened organizations have realized that and have started to look at these micro practices to ensure that women can work on career-advancing projects or get stretch assignments that develop their leadership skills.[8] Others have started to ensure that bias is not creeping into evaluations. However, changing gender patterns takes time. It also requires organizations to not only focus on changing women but also on changing the system of how organizations work.

With this gender binary understanding in mind, it is then not surprising that men will have a major role to play in gender equality processes. Men have gender, too, and they suffer from the current gender system as well. For instance the gender system requires men to the strong, powerful and heroic. This dominance has to be shown in competition which ascertains who is the Alpha Male. These are forms of what is called hegemonic masculinity, a dominant form of masculinity that subjugates other masculinities and all femininities.[9] Men who perform hegemonic masculinity are required to provide for their families, which in turn requires not only a steady job but also steady career progression with the associated salary increase. Organizations recognize this for instance in the fact that there is a 'daddy bonus' – men who become fathers often receive a salary boost to ensure that they can provide financially for their families.[10] However, men are not only conceptualized as financial providers; if they aim to be care providers and take paternity leave this is often met with surprise, mockery and the allegation of laziness.[11] While parts of the current gender system are privileging men, the constant need to financially provide and win competitions to progression is not something that all men enjoy.

While part of reshaping gender in organizations means to focus on recognizing and valuing men's changing roles in society, men also have a major role to play inside the workplace itself. Men can be change markers for gender equality through their daily interactions and advocacy for gender equality. Change makers for gender equality can be embedded in institutional roles. For instance, diversity and inclusion professionals can be seen as change agents for gender equality where creating gender equality is part of the job remit and which often requires individuals to influence without much authority. However, change markers for gender equality can be found anywhere in the organization from the CEO right down to frontline service staff.

Generally, women and men can act as change agents. However, depending on who is enacting change agency the effects will be rather different. Research has shown that women who are change agents for gender equality are less effective because it is presumed that they are engaging in the change processes for instrumental reasons.[12] It is presumed that women are advocates for gender equality because this can advance their own career. However, women might also not advance gender equality because they do not feel a sense of belonging to women as a group.[13] Men in contrast are seen as more effective advocates for gender equality for the opposite reasons. Their engagement is seen as altruistic because they do not seek to advance their own career opportunities. While men can actually advance their careers through being change makers for gender,[14] the common perception is that men are change markers for gender equality without expecting personal gains. If men engage in gender equality this might also be a particularly powerful statement because someone from the majority is driving change on behalf of a group that has been disempowered. This makes men particularly effective as change agents.

In sum, if we want to change gender relations in organizations, it is not enough to focus on women and developing them as leaders. There needs to be a focus on men, too. In particular there is an urgent need to reflect on how men can become and act as change markers for gender equality given the fact that they seem to hold particular power in regard to making changes happen.

Men and gender equality: perpetrator or champion?

"Women should not be seen as victims." This is what the CEO of a Fast-Moving Consumer Goods (FMCG) company said when I led a training for his group of senior leaders. In his view, movements like #MeToo position women as victims which takes away their agency. What struck me is that if women are the victims then men are constructed as the perpetrators. It is not only the lack of women's agency that is problematic, but it is also a role that men are assigned as perpetrators that is important here. It is also problematic to cast men in the role of heroes when we use the language of men as champions for gender equality. As I will suggest in this section, neither the idea that men are perpetuators nor the idea that men are champions is entirely useful when thinking about gender equality.

Men are often given a limited number of roles when it comes to gender equality. For example they might make an appearance as supportive husbands. It has long been argued that women's lives have transformed substantially in the last decades with women being increasingly visible in leadership while men's lives have transformed to a lesser degree. Men are still seen as providers for the family unit and are expected to be heroic and competitive in the workplace. While women's roles in society have changed, men's roles are only changing slowly. If men are not involved in change processes, it is very difficult to change gender relations! Yet many discussions on men and gender equality seem to recur to traditional frames of gender inequalities where men are largely blamed for perpetuating gender inequality or alternatively seem to carve out positions for men that construct them as victims of an ideology that seeks to advance gender equality. I suggest that neither frame of reference is useful.

The recent focus on sexual harassment in the context of the #MeToo movement has highlighted the role that men play in maintaining the current gender system. However, it had rather unexpected effects in the workplace: a common reaction of men is to refuse to support women in the workplace. I, for instance, heard many men who refused to become a mentor to women due to the perceived risk of being accused of harassing women. This appears like an extreme reaction and begs the question if men struggle to understand the boundaries between supporting women and harassing them. It also gives rise to the idea that men are the new victims of gender because anything they do can be used against them. Men are constructed as harassing women, being obsolete and being hindered in their own career due to the focus on promoting women. We certainly saw such perspectives in our research with women and men who aspire to board roles where men suggested that their own lack of success in attaining a board role is due to the fact that women now appear as preferred candidates to join boards.[15] This was in spite of the fact that the majority of board roles during the time of the study still went to men.

If we look at much of the research on men and gender equality, it is notable that it documents how men perpetuate gender inequalities through their actions. Earlier research has shown how men systematically undermine women.[16] For instance, men might challenge events that are organized to support women. Similarly, men act in concert to exclude women, men are sucking up to other men with the hope of advancing their career, and men gang up on women to eliminate competition from them.[17] These processes are largely subconscious although some might men use these tactics consciously. They serve to perpetuate gender inequalities and are often part of unreflected practices that are re-enacted without much reflection. It is important to note that this research acknowledges that these actions are guided by the existing gender system. While this is often read as blaming men for gender inequality, a more useful frame of reference is to acknowledge that men engage in establishing gender inequality but that often happens unintentionally.

Currently, we see attempts to bring men into the discussions about gender inequalities by describing them as 'champions'. Alternatively, the word 'allies' is used. While those attempts have good intentions, the language that is being used is at best misleading. A champion can be an advocate or a supporter of a cause, but the use of champions also invokes sporting language where a winner is taking it all and gets a medal for this. While this is designed to appeal to men, it equally recreates expected gender norms, and it also introduces notions of competitiveness that means that some people win, and others lose. Using champions in the context of gender equality is then easily translated into that either women or men win the 'battles of the sexes'. This is less useful to advance discussions. Similarly, talking about allies suggests that men support a cause, which is not related to themselves. Gender is thereby constructed as something for women where men have no active involvement in. Men have as much interest in the gender system as women and should therefore have a central shaping role, too. It invokes notions of chivalry, gallantry and gentlemanliness where a damsel-in-distress has to be rescued by a male hero. Again those images might not be entirely useful to reflect on men's role in gender equality.

Even though many men perceive their career chances as reduced, overall the gender system is still stacked in favour of men. This is counteracting the common sentiment in society that we are self-responsible for creating our own success but also have to shoulder the risk of failure. The sociological term for this process is individualization.[18] We do not expect or in fact like the idea that gender, class or race would determine our life chances. However, due to the gender system outlined previously, it is men who profit from the current arrangements; this has been called 'patriarchal dividend'.[19] This does not mean that men are not subject to the restrictions of the current gender system but that they implicitly benefit from it. However, this specific position in the gender system also means that they can be change agents for gender equality.

The change-maker framework

"I cannot be a change agent for gender equality, Elisabeth, I do not have any daughters" said Sandro who was a managing partner in a professional services company. He had received negative feedback about his perceived lack of support for gender equality in the firm. He was not against gender equality as such but every time he tried to engage on the issue, his involvement was described as lacklustre. Someone from Human Resources (HR) found him a coach to support him on how to be more impactful in his engagement for gender equality. However, the coaching session left Sandro with the impression that in order to be authentic in regard to gender equality you need to be a father of daughters and he had sons. While it is correct that many men who are change agents for gender equality refer to their daughters, wives and mothers as a reason why they got interested in the subject,[20] it is clearly not the only way in which men can become change agents for gender equality. As a matter of fact, everyone who wants to become a change maker can do that. In this book I suggest that the path of the change maker is a framework which can be used to act and think like a change agent for gender equality.

So far we have seen how leadership means taking others with you on a path and how this journey can be seen as a change process. Leadership and change are of course related. But how can we conceptualize change and why is it so important for leadership and for gender equality? Let's say you want to change the shape of an ice cube. Currently the ice cube is in a cubical shape, but you want an ice ball. The obvious course of action is to unfreeze your cube and refreeze it in an ice ball shape. This is akin what one of the best-known models for change proposed. The change model, often attributed to Lewin, conceptualizes change as unfreezing, change and refreezing.[21] Like an ice cube the ice is molten into water and this water is then poured into a new ice tray that has a different shape and refrozen to form ice cubes that are shaped in a new way. This deceivingly straightforward model of change allows us to see how change can happen. However, in reality these processes are more complex, and we know that change processes are often going to be resisted and challenged.

This is where change agents – or as I prefer to call them change makers – come in. Change agents are individuals who drive change in an organizational context. Change agents are individuals who often work outside of the formal structure and without formal authority to drive change projects.[22] They work across established boundaries and organizational silos to make change happen. Very often they do their work through convincing others. They are passionate about the change but also respect that change takes time. As a change maker you have to convince others of the importance of gender equality, be passionate about this topic but also respect that others might take longer to join you on the path.

Why some people become change markers and others do not is not straightforward. Some individuals are imbued with the professional capacity to make change happen. For instance, many senior leaders like CEOs promise specific changes before they are appointed and then drive those as well as other changes during their tenure as a CEO. A middle manager might take up a change project to show her ability to lead change and thus move up the organizational ladder. Alternatively, you might be passionate about an area such as sustainability and seek out ways to make your organization more environmentally friendly. Or you could be an activist who is hired by an organization to create inclusion for people identifying as lesbian, gay, bisexual, transgender, queer/questioning (LGBTQ). It is also possible that you simply take on a change project to advance your career but end up becoming passionate about the subject matter. If you are a change maker, you have a vision about how a field should transform and work with others to make this a reality. Change makers show others the path of how to create transformation and others are moved to follow that path. Change makers enact leadership.

I have suggested earlier that changes related to gender relations require a more sustained effort due to the deep-rooted gender beliefs in society. Yet, creating more gender equality can also become part of your legacy where you leave an imprint on the organization after you are no longer there.

But if you decide to become a change maker for gender equality, how do you start? I have organized the change-maker framework into three parts: visioning, enabling and modelling. If you want others to join you on a path you need to convince them that you have an idea where you are going. This requires vision. Vision is central for leaders because as a follower you are more likely to follow leaders if you see their vision as worthwhile to pursue. The first step is then to develop your vision. You need to reflect on why you personally support gender equality and what gender equality looks like. There are many approaches and definitions out there that you can use, and I will share them later on, but you need to decide which ones are the most relevant and convincing for you. Once you have found your vision, you then need to articulate it. If you have your vision and do not share it with others, it will be difficult for them to follow you. You need to find your own voice to be a change maker for gender equality.

You found your vision and are able to articulate it. Now it is time to use your voice in the organization by enabling gender equality. Enabling does not mean that you need to spend most of your days dedicated to gender equality. That would not be realistic or in fact desirable. Your role as a leader is to facilitate an environment where others can take action. Yes in some cases this will involve you driving a new initiative for gender equality but in others you might create the biggest impact by lending your weight to what the organization already does. Enabling first means that you need to seek out situations where you can make a difference. This often involves putting yourself in the shoes of others and seeing the world from their perspective. You can use these insights to amplify their perspective and create understanding in others. Your role is also going to entail dealing with those who resist gender equality. This can be in overt forms by actively opposing gender equality or more convert forms such as simply not caring for it.

The third part of the change maker framework is modelling. How you behave will influence how others act on gender equality. You might articulate a vision on gender equality but if you do not practice what you preach your ability to become a change agent for gender equality is going to be limited. What does that mean in practice? It means that you need to disrupt practices that create gender inequality. If a woman is not listened to in a meeting, you might want to repeat the point and attribute it to the woman. If you see that people are hiring people like themselves, point this out. It can mean to mentor and sponsor women or to congratulate colleagues on their gender equality efforts.

As you will have noticed, I used gerund forms to describe the three parts of the change-maker model. This is intentional because what I describe are practices that you are doing and refining over time. Visioning, enabling and modelling thus are three essential practices associated with becoming a change maker for gender equality. Each of these practices is discussed in turn. Each chapter will also feature some suggestions on how you can improve the respective activity. While I described the model as a path to align with how I define leadership, the path is a twisting and winding one. The book and framework are not laid out as a linear trajectory but as a matter of what you might imagine as more like 'Snakes and Ladders'.[23] Sometimes you advance quickly but other times you are sliding back. For instance, you might develop your vision for creating gender equality, but you revise it later on. I would suggest reading the book in a linear way, starting with visioning, enabling and modelling. This will give you a good overview of what you could consider when becoming a change maker for gender equality. However, you might at specific points in time want to revisit individual chapters like on enabling if you feel you need to reinvigorate your leadership in that respect.

Are you ready to step forward on the path of gender-inclusive leadership?

1. Leadership is inviting others to follow you on a path. Gender-inclusive leadership means taking others with us on the path to gender equality.
2. Gender equality is often conceived as something for women. Yet gender is about men and women.
3. How gender expresses itself in your organization is intertwined with how gender is organized in society at large. Most efforts to

create more gender equality fail because gender is understood in too narrow and simplified ways.

4. This results, for instance, in the fact that women and men can be change agents for leadership, but men are particularly effective in this role.

2
VISIONING

After having listened to one of the senior leaders in her organization talk about his commitment to gender equality, Laura remarked to me that "he really lacks a vision for gender equality". The senior leader had spoken about the business case for women in general terms. Like so many other leaders, he reiterated the standard research findings how gender equality is good for business. Yet for Laura something was missing. He was missing a vision. I probe what she would like to see to which Laura responds "I would like to see why he personally is involved in gender equality and how he sees gender equality evolve in the organization". The temptation to use data to convince others that gender equality makes business sense is strong but what most followers would want to hear is a vision for gender equality.

Visioning is the activity of thinking about the future and planning a path towards this future. As a leader, you are required to develop a vision of where you want to go, and your followers will follow you because they see this vision as desirable. For this to happen you obviously first need to develop a vision. You then need to paint a picture for others of what the future might look like. You need to communicate your vision or in other words you need to find your voice. This is the focus of this chapter.

"I want my daughters to work in a workplace where they do not experience gender inequality" was a common statement by CEOs when they articulated their support for gender equality. In the previous chapter we met Sandro who felt that he could not be an advocate for gender equality because he did not have any daughters. In part having daughters would allow Sandro to develop a compelling reason why he is supporting gender equality: he wants his daughters to work in a workplace that is more gender equality. The use of daughters to signal support for gender equality is a clear vision for gender equality. Any follower would immediately understand why a senior leader is committed to gender equality and how a future where gender equality is achieved would look.

Developing a vision is a deeply personal endeavour because your vision has to resonate with who you are as person. Hence the reference to daughters. However, these are not the only reasons you can use to develop your vision for gender equality.

The business case, the fairness case and the personal case

When asked how he became a supporter for gender equality, Oscar responded that is all goes back to a book.

> 'I read this book which touched me deeply. The book showed how gender inequality is deeply engrained in societies and how this is holding societies back. Moving towards gender equality is the right thing to do for reasons of social fairness. And as a business leader, I learned that it is good for business too!'

Oscar is describing here an epiphany moment when reading a book changed his outlook. He is not only describing a social fairness case but also links this to the business case.

Normally, leaders and particularly men in leadership positions offer three reasons why they are engaged in gender equality. Those three reasons – or cases – are often used to explain their support for gender equality and most leaders draw on several cases simultaneously.

Interestingly, the first case is the one that is most prevalent: the business case. While it is interesting to note that the business case is the most common one, it is probably not surprising. Traditionally there was the expectation that organizations only engage in gender equality if there is a good business reason why they should. This gave rise to a whole range of businesses cases for gender equality. For instance, it is common to make the case that women should be on boards because this improves the functioning of boards.[1] This is a version of the business case. We have also shown in research that having 50 per cent women and 50 per cent men in a team leads to an environment that is ideal for innovation.[2] If your organization seeks innovation, then gender parity in teams makes business sense.

These examples illustrate that for the last 15 to 20 years the business case for gender equality has been made in a variety of shapes and forms. At this historic moment in time, there was a sense that leaders need to understand why gender equality is important and making a business argument was seen as most convincing. As such this is what many leaders repeat when asked about their support for gender equality. They talk about studies that have shown how having gender equality can improve business outcomes.

The second case for gender equality centres on fairness. Organizations do the 'right thing'. For instance the United Nations' Sustainable Development Goals (SDGs) focus on achieving gender equality and empowering women and girls. Gender equality is also mainstreamed in all other goals. These SDGs are regularly used in organizations to justify their engagement on gender equality. Achieving gender equality is then a question of social fairness. This perspective is also mobilized when discussing the reasons for getting involved in gender equality. Improving the bottom line is as much a central feature of achieving gender equality as doing the right thing.

The epiphany moment described in the beginning of this chapter is a typical example of recognizing the importance of gender equality in the wider context of social fairness, social responsibility and social sustainability. Such epiphany moments were often defining in the journey to becoming a leader for gender equality.

The third case, the personal case, is also often related to an epiphany moment but it is in many cases more personal. Let's look at how the person case for Adam evolved. Adam worked in a German manufacturing organization. The company maintained a social environment and many colleagues would spend time together after work such as going for a beer. He had joined such outings many times and found them invaluable to develop his network. While touring the German operations he met Gülce who was a junior woman from a Turkish-German background. He asked her if Gülce would join them after work for a little get together. Gülce was taken aback. Adam wondered if he said something wrong. However, Gülce was surprised to be invited and recounted that this is the first time in her almost four years in the company that she had been invited for an after-hours meeting. Adam asked why that was the case. Gülce responded that this had never been made explicit, but she had her assumptions. She sensed that colleagues did not invite her to join them after hours because they presumed that she did not drink alcohol, was not allowed to go out without a chaperon or had caring responsibilities. She talked about how these unspoken assumptions meant that she was not even invited to join her colleagues and as a consequence regularly was surprised by decisions that had been taken during after hour meetings. It had never crossed Adam's mind that the after-hours socializing could be exclusionary if some people are not even invited to join in. This epiphany moment motivated Adam to schedule social get-togethers during work time from then on.

The epiphany is a common feature in how leaders talk about their engagement in gender equality efforts. They might have had a specific experience like in Adam's case, they might have read a book that made the point why gender equality is important, or they might have other personal reasons. Not surprisingly the most commonly cited relates to having a daughter and realizing as a consequence that gender equality is important. However, other leaders cited their mothers and aunts as inspirations for getting serious about gender equality. Overall, referring to 'strong women' in their life was a common feature of the discussions.

The good news is that having strong women is only one way of developing a personal case for gender equality. Rashid for instance has experienced being different from the norm because he is from an ethnic minority background in the country he works in. He told me how he noticed that he became very mindful of where he sits at a table to avoid being excluded from the discussion. He said that he has talked about this with women who are also vigilant about where they sit in a meeting to give them the best chance of being heard. Rashid commented that he never heard a majority group man reflect on such issues and he speculated that rather than being heard, majority group men select seats in a meeting as a subconscious decision to exert power. For those who are different, it is a question of being heard. Rashid through his experiences of being different thus had a nuanced understanding of what it feels like to be excluded and used this insight to ensure greater inclusion among women, too.

Although the business case and fairness case for gender equality are important, it is the personal case for gender equality that is likely to have the biggest impact for convincing to follow you on the path.

Three ways to think about men as change agents

I was chatting to Luke, who was in the C-suite in his organization, about why he thought that men were hesitant to be change makers for gender equality. Luke said, "Dying for a higher cause – no one really likes that". He elaborated that men are asked to make a sacrifice for the fact that women were historically disadvantaged. Men are now asked to undo past inequalities. This implicitly means that men are required to give up their own chances of progressing in the organization. Luke suggested that many men he spoke with found this unfair. Why should their give up career opportunities to create gender equality? This 'dying for a higher cause' was not attractive to most men.

This conversation points to another important aspect when thinking about men as change agents for gender equality. How are men discussed in relation to gender equality in an organization? Most organizations have now developed ways to involve men in gender equality yet how men are conceptualized varies and that matters for how they can position themselves. It does not mean that you have to take up this position but becoming aware of how men are talked about in relation to gender equality is certainly important in that process.

In my own research, I have documented three ways in which men are talked about in gender equality processes.[3] I called these 'personas' the inclusive leader, the smart strategist, and the forced altruist. In many ways they are extremes illustrating potential ways men are talked about. These personas are not exclusive and potentially many more exist. However, they give an illustration of how men are talked about. What they do not give information on is how men position themselves in regard to those personas. It is useful to consider these personas to allow you to carve out a position that you wish to adopt.

The inclusive leader is possibly the most common persona when men are being talked about in gender equality discourses. What goes into the construction of the inclusive leader? First, the inclusive leader needs to be educated on biases. Bias awareness training is a central strategy for many diversity and inclusion programmes although their effectiveness is contested.[4] These bias awareness trainings are established with the idea in mind that if people are educated on their biases, they would be better able to address them. A consequence for men as change agents is that they are expected to talk about biases and to address them through their daily activities. For instance the inclusive leader might learn that we prefer to hang out with people who are more similar to ourselves. The inclusive leader might counteract that bias by consciously building a team of people who are different from himself. Rather than hiring people who went to the same university as him or play the same sports, he is actively seeking out those who are different, such as not attending a university at all or not playing any sports. The ability to be an inclusive leader also means to challenge others on their own behaviour. For example, when talking about promotions, it is the role of the inclusive leader to disrupt biases in others by discussing the strength of individuals who might be different from the norm. Inclusion is here seen as a way to improve organizational functioning because it allows for the inclusion of different people into decision-making processes. The inclusive leadership persona thus focuses on leaders who are encouraged to improve their decision making through inclusion.

The smart strategist is another persona that emerged in my research. While the inclusive leader is trying to correct for bias in decision making, the focus of the smart strategist is on the business value that gender equality brings. The inclusive leader focuses on improving decision making whereas the smart strategist focuses on making strategic choices. This often includes an awareness that gender equality is important for two reasons: first, talent includes both men and women, and second, customers can be men and women, too. Gender equality is increasingly seen as the smart thing to participate in to attract customers and talent. As such, many organizations have started to discuss gender equality in terms of business opportunities. This echoes the business case that we earlier encountered as a rationale for why men engage in gender equality. It might for instance be that if senior leadership decides that gender equality is strategically important, gender equality is then included as a criterion in performance evaluations. Employees are asked to show how they made strategic choices that support gender equality.

An example includes the sales strategy in the company. One manager, Dimitri, noticed that incentives for sales representatives were tailored towards men – literally tailored because if you did well in sales you received a tie! However, this ignored the rising numbers of women in sales. The manager might have decided to simply find another incentive for women such as a scarf. However, instead he decided to speak to women working sales and it turned out that a scarf was not particularly attractive either. Dimitri also found out that other events organized as rewards had the feeling of a whiskey-and-cigar club and were not comfortable spaces for women. Dimitri realized that the problem went much deeper than just the ties and embarked on a journey to reinvent the incentive structure for salespeople to be more inclusive. Dimitri made a number of changes; it should be noted that the tie gift was replaced by vouchers which allowed people to select their preferred incentive and events were focused on experiences such as inviting a chef for a cooking experience or a yoga and well-being event. Much to his surprise, he noticed that not only were more women attracted to work in sales, the sales figures also improved. Dimitri was rewarded with a promotion for being a smart strategist in relation to gender equality.

Earlier on we met Luke who talked about how men are expected to die for a higher cause when supporting gender equality. I have this persona, the 'forced altruist'. Whereas the previous two personas were largely found in commercial organizations, the forced altruist is possibly a more likely construction in public sector and international organizations. The reason for this might be that such organizations are often guided by a stronger higher cause or social justice motive, such as improving the world. In such organizations it is commonly stressed that historically men were more present in the public sphere, which has led to leadership imbalances. In order to correct these imbalances, so the reasoning goes, it is necessary for women to be advantaged over men. For example, in regard to hiring and promotion women might be preferred. This implicitly means that men are less likely to get hired or to advance because women are now preferred. In other words, men are asked to make a personal sacrifice in terms of their career advancement to allow women to take on leadership positions. Not surprisingly, such reasoning will draw a lot of resentment from men. Even if men agree that women are disadvantaged, being asked to give up your own career ambitions for the greater good of gender equality might be a hard pill to swallow. Such a stance will likely cause a lot of resentment. It is often mentioned in the same breath as having a mandatory quota for women, which likewise causes a lot of debate.[5]

It is interesting to note that the first two personas appeal much more to what is in it for men to engage in gender equality. Both the inclusive leader and the smart strategist are linked to opportunities that arise out of the engagement for gender equality. For instance, your promotion might be contingent on showing these desired practices for gender equality. The forced altruist in contrast is asked to sacrifice his own career to advance gender equality in general. Whereas the other two personas transformed engagement for gender equality into individual career success for men, here men are constructed as losing out. Their personal career will not flourish.

In my research I have shown that men who engage in gender equality regularly reap the benefits of such behaviour,[6] but I also found that the idea that men need to give up something for gender equality is often resurfacing. As such it has to be discussed and addressed rather than ignored. By for instance stressing personal career benefits of engaging in gender equality it is possible to counteract the perception that men lose out when gender equality is worked towards.

How men as change agents are talked about in organizations is thus an important consideration for how you articulate your vision for gender equality. While you might not agree with the framing in your organization, you could at least use it as a starting point to articulate how you see your role as a change agent. Are you an inclusive leader who tries to create inclusion by building diverse teams? Are you a smart strategist who tries to orient decisions towards diverse talent and customers? Or are you positioned as a forced altruist giving up your career to allow women to succeed? In reality you might want to mix-and-match these positions to find something that fits you well.

Beyond the hero

I am sitting with Sally in a cafe after an event we attended together, and Sally tells me about how she experienced her own leadership journey. One of the most remarkable changes in her view is that when she started out in finance in the 1990s, you had to be tough as nails. Show no emotion. Be ruthless. Be greedy. Just like Gordon Gekko in the movie Wall Street she said. However, when she now attends leadership seminars it is all about emotional intelligence and empathy. One is encouraged to be soft. However, Sally found this difficult as a woman because she tried her entire working life to appear as not too emotional. She explained that she wanted to escape the common gender stereotype that women are touchy-feely and cannot make tough calls. Sally acknowledges two things: first that the ideal of leadership has changed and second that as a woman this new form of leadership is difficult to inhabit.

I will focus on the first part of her realization – that leadership has changed and what that means for men as leaders for gender equality. Sally's astute observation that leadership has turned to social-emotional skills is something academic research has also uncovered. In academic research this is called post-heroic leadership.[7] Before delving into post-heroic leadership, we first need to determine what heroic leadership is. Early leadership theories focused on the leader as a 'great man'.[8] The great man theory of leadership postulates that leaders are born not made. More specifically, some people are born with the right attributes to lead others. Many of those attributes are linked to being heroic and this heroism was often equated with bravery akin to that displayed on a battlefield. Those heroes were admired by others for how tough and aggressive they were and how they took charge in challenging situations. All of these expectations still reverberate today in what we expect leaders to be. All of those characteristics are also associated with men in general in society.

How men in general are perceived in society is often described as masculinity. Masculinity is a collection of assumptions, traits and perceptions that align with how men are expected to be and behave. It is a generalized notion of what men in societies are like. A first observation is that of course not all men conform to this idealized masculinity. In fact, very few men do.[9] There are huge variations how men behave: some men behave in hegemonic masculine ways and want to dominate others[10] whereas other men might display more caring masculinities by offer support for others.[11] In spite of those differences in how masculinity is performed, society expects masculinity in men. Second, these expectations vary culturally both historically and geographically. While today pink is commonly associated with girls, historically the colour pink was presumed to signify virility and masculinity and was used for boys.[12] Similarly, competitiveness is often linked to men but it has been shown that competitiveness can relate to the position one occupies in society where competitiveness might be required.[13] This variability of what is associated with masculinity and by extension men is thus an indication that what we presume to be masculinity is in fact socially constructed.

However, masculinity being socially constructed does not mean that it does not have real effects. Women like Sally regularly are measured against the ideal of what men are supposed to be like as leaders in organizations. She has to be masculine to be perceived as a leader, which is why she is hesitant to show socio-emotional skills because those are seen as feminine. If she appears as too feminine, she might not be seen as a leader after all. However, she probably has to show a bit of femininity to appear as a woman. A true balancing act on a tight rope!

So how has leadership changed in recent decades? Sally is right to observe that leadership has focused more on skills that are no longer associated with masculine notions of being tough, ruthless and self-interested. Leadership focused on command and control. However, newer forms of leadership are based on shared decision making and agreeing action in a collaborative fashion. Everyone can make a contribution and is heard. Leadership now involves supporting others in their development and engaging in coaching and mentoring others. Leaders are less interested in glory for themselves but are open to sharing glory with others. They also do not need to appear as knowing it all but are open to asking questions about areas they are less certain about. Now leaders are not constantly talking but make space for others to speak and they are skilled in listening to others. Similarly they are not afraid to make and admit to mistakes rather than to appear as flawless. They do not need to appear as constantly fighting a battle and pushing themselves and others to the limit. Instead of dominating others, they might show humility. They use emotional intelligence rather than simply relying on rational arguments. Gone are competitive sports or battle metaphors and instead new leaders might talk about their commitments and enjoyments in private life.[14] All of this is part of what is called post-heroic leadership.[15] Much of how we envision leaders is still rooted in traditional heroic notions. Being a hero means to face challenging situations with courage. Ideally we expect the hero to succeed in the end. Like a hero leaders are expected to tackle tricky situations, have some sort of success and be admired for this. This traditional notion of the hero is often strongly related to masculinity as discussed previously.

Even though we see the rise of post-heroic leadership as a different approach to lead, it is interesting to note that when men are encouraged to support gender equality at work, the same heroic discourse is often used. For instance, as mentioned earlier, men are often discussed as champions who are celebrated for their support for women. Such language is used to entice more men to be active on gender equality. Yet this language recurs to rather traditional notions of heroic leadership. Not only is this idea old-fashioned but it also invokes traditional notions of masculinity. As such, describing men as change agents as heroic champions risks cementing masculine ideals about leadership. It is also anachronistic in light of the rise of post-heroic leadership. Casting men who engage on gender equality as heroes is thus limiting the emancipatory power that such roles can entail. As such, becoming a post-heroic leader is closely aligned with being a true change maker for gender equality.

Articulating your vision

Claus has been appointed as the CEO of a global organization. During his career which spans decades in the field, he continually expanded his leadership skills and was generally confident that he counts as a good leader and that he can inspire others. He is no stranger to challenging discussions and has developed the strategy of standing his ground to emerge from those discussions victorious. While the verdict on his leadership is largely positive, the feedback he received from a woman's day event where he spoke at was devastating. Claus thought that he had done a good job. He made time in his busy diary to attend the event and made some remarks to open the event. Claus made the effort to stay for the entire event rather than departing early. Yet the feedback from the event was not good at all and caused some concern for Claus personally but also for his chief of HR. Claus was flabbergasted that his intervention had not gone down well. It turned out that in spite of working with competent women for most of his career, he still saw women as a mix of his own mother and his wife rather than as a professional equal. Claus sensed that his life experience would limit his ability to come across well at women's day events.

We saw a similar moment earlier in relation to the statement that many men make: 'as a father of a daughter'. 'As the father of a daughter' seems like an intuitive and believable thing to say. And it might be why you realized the importance of gender in the first place. As a matter of fact some research claims that fathers of daughters hold less traditional gender attitudes; researchers have termed this the 'mighty girl' effect.[16]

However, I have seen that many audiences are immediately switched off by this statement. Daughters are often used to disclaim that men are sexist, which does not appear particularly convincing because simply being related to a woman will not eradicate sexist behaviour. It is also unclear why the sympathetic feeling you have towards your daughter, should rub off onto other women who you know professionally. The relationships are going to be very different by their very nature. There is also another fallacy – you liken your daughter to a woman you are working with professionally. It is as if you speak to a senior women's event of women in their

40s, 50s and 60s and liken their experience of the workplace to your daughter who at 19 is just doing her first internship. This is somewhat disregarding the years of experience that the senior women have accumulated. If your daughter is younger, it risks infantilizing women in the workplace. Finally, it also seems to create uncomfortable resonances with patriarchy, which means the law of the father who is in charge, in control and also protects women. It risks mobilizing chivalrous images of women who need to be protected and rescued. Referring to daughters is therefore probably not the best strategy to use.

Let's unpack this idea of being a father of daughters a bit more. In conversations this reference is often used to give the speaker credibility – they know what they are talking about. But what does it actually imply? Did an awareness of gender equality just arise with the birth of a daughter or when the daughter entered the workplace? What exactly made the father think about gender equality in this context? Was he unaware of gender inequality before or did it simply not matter to him? Does a father of a daughter suddenly become an expert on gender equality and all things women? Would it not be more convincing to provide a specific example of how you realized the importance of gender equality beyond your immediate family environment? It is clear to see that there are limitations to this rhetorical device to invoke daughters. However, why it is used is because it is supposed to show why gender equality matters to this person. There is a multitude of other ways to achieve that go beyond invoking being the father of a daughter. What is key is rather to link your support for gender equality to a personal story.

Why is this personal story so important? One reason is that men are generally perceived as unaffected by gender inequalities. Gender inequalities are seen as relating to women. As such women have a presumed self-interest in supporting gender equality; they can profit from it. For men the reason why they engage in gender equality is not obvious. On the face of it, they have nothing to gain from gender equality. Conventional thinking rather suggests that they have much to lose because they need to give up something. Men's engagement in gender equality is not something obvious and thus requires explanation. A good story of why you personally care for gender equality is therefore required.

While this explanation for an engagement in gender equality has to be provided by men, the need to justify one's engagement with gender equality efforts as a man goes beyond that. It also indicates that people want to know leaders personally. They want to know who leaders are before they follow them.[17] It relates to authentic leadership, which refers to leaders who appear as true to themselves.[18] They live their values and take others on the path with them. As a matter of fact, being able to articulate their values is key to taking others with them on the path.

Getting the buy-in to join you on the path is especially relevant for efforts around something as difficult to grasp as gender equality. Gender equality is by many still seen as lying outside of normal responsibilities that an organization has – namely to strive and thrive by fulfilling its purpose. Gender equality is therefore seen as 'discretionary' and potentially part of wider corporate responsibilities, but not as something that is core to what an organization does. This is why it takes convincing. Convincing can often happen through storytelling. Storytelling is commonly assumed to speak to individuals on an intellectual and emotional level. Leaders are regularly advised to tell stories to communicate a vision.[19] The same holds true for communicating a certain image about themselves.

So how can you voice your vision for gender equality? First, think beyond daughters and instead think about events where you realized the importance of gender equality within the workplace, such as through women you work with. One senior leader for instance had a female boss early in his career and uses these interactions as an example of how he realized the importance of gender. Another leader talked about how he learned through a mentee what it meant to juggle childcare arrangements. Yet another leader talked about his female peer in another organization and how she diffused a challenging situation through diplomacy and remained focused, thus avoiding a major disaster. Or you could think about telling a story about a man who did not get it and who you convinced of the importance of gender equality.

Second, avoid stereotypes in your stories or blanket statements. It is particularly tempting to use benevolent stereotypes in your stories because after all they are there to make women appear good and that it what you want to achieve. However, your audience will see right through that. Many people will simply switch off because you use a cliché rather than something more novel. It is easy to recur to stereotypes in your stories but not only are they boring they will also limit your effectiveness. Instead, try to find stories that are unusual and are counterintuitive. This will also enhance that people can recall the story later on.

Third, do not always tell the same story. Instead, find different stories and adapt them to the specific situation. Normally having three stories is great because this gives you enough material to choose from while also creating familiarity with the story in relation to those who might hear it more than once.

Fourth, developing your stories on why you support gender equality will take practice. You should practise your story and adapt it based on feedback. A coach or critical friend might be a good partner in the process who can listen to your stories and retell them for you to enhance the rhetorical effectiveness.

Fifth, you can use your stories to make it clear what your vision for gender equality in the organization is. You could for instance tell a story of how gender inequality currently manifests, why you think that is problematic and how you expect it to change. This vision will not require you to set out a specific plan or initiative of how to get there. Rather, your vision will be description of how you expect working in a more gender equal organization will feel like.

Communicating your vision

Developing your compelling story or rather stories of why you are engaged in gender equality is a core activity for leaders to communicate their vision for gender equality. Consider the following in regard to inspirational story telling for gender inclusion:

1. Tell stories about women, who you worked with and who inspired you.
2. Find counter-stereotypical stories.
3. Have a range of stories and adapt them to the situation.
4. Practise your stories to fine-tune them.
5. Make your stories visionary.

3
ENABLING

"I find it deeply unfair that I do not have a future in this company." Mario was angry. He had been working in the company for well over a decade and was ready to take the next big step by getting a promotion to manage a sizeable team. He felt that he ticked all the boxes for the promotion. So why did he sense that he does not have a future in the company? The company started a campaign to increase women in leadership positions. Like many organizations, this organization suffered from what is called the leaky pipeline. The leaky pipeline is a commonly used metaphor to describe that while women are present in entry-level position, they are underrepresented in leadership roles.[1] As such the organization decided to introduce a target – at least 40 per cent of promotions had to go to women. Mario thus felt that his chances of getting a promotion had evaporated and instead a woman who is less qualified than him would get ahead. Mario was frustrated and made this known in the company.

As a change maker for gender equality, you need to be prepared to deal with such resistance to gender equality. This is a key part of creating an enabling environment for inclusion. Dealing with resistance through empathy is also a core skill for the gender inclusive change maker.

Female advantage, men's disadvantage?

The change maker for gender equality will encounter resistance to gender equality efforts in many shapes and forms. Some believe that efforts around gender equality and diversity more widely are misguided and have gone too far. While these ideas have existed for a long time, they are increasingly voiced in the open. It reflects a feeling in part of the population that they are not given the same opportunities as other people. In this case it is often men who complain that women have the edge in regard to recruitment and promotion whereas men are now disadvantaged.

This relates to arguments that are aligned with the 'female advantage'. In our research we have shown how this argument is regularly used to suggest that women have an advantage because they are in a minority position in most workplaces, particularly in senior roles.[2] Since many organizations aim to increase the number of women in leadership women have a perceived advantage to get there. Women are often presumed to just be in senior roles to 'tick a box'. This is particularly strong when the woman is also non-white and not heterosexual.

With many organizations aiming to improve equality, being able to fill a position with a woman is seen as self-evident because it fulfils the implicit or explicit 'rule' that women should be advanced. This is constructed as having benefits in terms of being hired but also in regard to being promoted. We have also suggested in our research that the female advantage argument is being used to disclaim the need for feminism or any further action to create gender equality.[3]

Women's resistance

One group that often resists efforts to create gender equality is women themselves. Women do not want to be a 'quota woman'. This is surprising to many men because they presume that women benefit from gender equality efforts and therefore should be supportive of them. However, for many women a focus on gender equality often means that they feel reduced to being a woman: they feel promoted due to the fact that they are women and not due to their performance. They do not feel that they truly merit being in that role. They feel that they lose respect from others. They are simply a token. Women might therefore resist efforts around gender equality because they fear that is supports the perception that they themselves are simply 'quota women'.

Women might also resist men engaging in gender equality as the following incident illustrates. After having worked remotely for a long time due to the pandemic, Gregory was really happy to have been invited to a networking event. It was a networking event for women, but the event was open to everyone. Gregory was looking forward to not only seeing colleagues in person but also to learning more about gender equality at his organization. Entering the room he immediately noticed that the make-up of the room is dramatically different to events he normally attended. More than 90 per cent of the attendees were women! He felt odd. Suddenly he was in a minority. This awkward feeling only increased once he tried to walk towards one of the many small groups of largely women that had formed in the room. He attempted to join one of these groups. But once he joined, the discussion stopped, and the women found excuses to circulate in the room. That was not the only time this happened during the evening.

Men might be surprised that many women dislike the fact that men become involved in gender equality. Many women feel that men have no space in discussions about gender equality. Some women resent that they are invited in to spaces that were designed for women such as women's networking events. This clearly chimes with Gregory's experience. However, networking is not the only space where this is an issue.

Torsten was excited for the birth of his first child. He was keen to be present during the birth and had a conversation with his boss Tabea how this could be managed. Tabea was clearly not pleased about this request and did not want to plan Torsten's workload in a way that would have allowed him the flexibility to be present during the birth of his child. Torsten was frustrated by this lack of understanding. Surely Tabea would understand the importance of such life events. She had after all fought hard to establish a women's network, which had become influential in the organization. Gender equality was extremely important for her. However, after many years of fighting for gender equality, she resented that men reap the benefit of these struggles. Tabea saw Torsten's request as such an incident and was as such not very supportive of it.

Lauren was attending a networking event and was pleased to see some men there. She saw a man standing on his own and decided to strike up a conversation. He introduced himself as Gregory (we met him at the beginning of this section) and after some small talk Lauren talked about a tricky situation in her team where her contribution was not appreciated. Gregory offered to help by talking to her boss. Lauren first felt that this was a generous offer. Yet she also felt slightly uncomfortable about this offer to help getting her the credit she deserves. It seemed like chivalry where Gregory rescued her from a difficult situation. She was certainly not a damsel-in-distress who needed to be rescued. Lauren understood the offer of help as patronizing. After careful consideration Lauren thanked Gregory for the offer but declined this politely. Instead she asked what he would do in that situation.

Some women react strongly to the suggestion that they need any support to advance in the workplace. They are led to believe that they can make it on their own. Requiring the help of someone else is not empowering and is contracting much advice that women get from self-help books. These self-help books claim that women can be successful as they are able to transform themselves into the ideal woman leader.[4] This can be achieved through a range of self-focused practices such as being more confident.[5] If it is suggested that you can be successful by transforming yourself, needing support from others might appear as disempowering. Some might react in particular to the chivalrous assumptions that women need men to save them. Women who want to appear as in charge of their own destiny will dislike the suggestion that they need the support of men to advance in their career. These women actively try to resist the construction of women as passive and instead try to claim agency to change their lives. As such, they might react negatively to being cast as a damsel-in-distress and might push back when they are offered help.

Diversity among women

Women might also disagree with the gender equality policies and practices put in place. There is considerable disagreement on which policies and practices work to create gender equality and individuals often have strong views on what needs to be done. For instance a mother of younger children might think that focusing on work-life integration measures is key while a woman from a working-class background is keen to bring more women from a working-class background into the organization. In academic terms this is often called essentializing women and this is generally not seen as a good thing. Essentializing means that you presume that women and men have specific essences that stay do not change.[6] It is very similar to using stereotypes or having biases cloud your judgement. While most organizations try to avoid biases and stereotypes because they put people into categories, it seems more acceptable to use the same stereotypes and biases if they are positive. For instance a number of CEOs talked about the social and emotional skills women bring to the workplace. While they often acknowledged the sweeping generalizations by statements such as 'I know it is a cliché to say that women are more in touch with their emotions' to then progress to use exactly this cliché in their argument ('But it is really my experience, that women are more emotionally competent'). While these stereotypes are well-meaning and well-intentioned, they still put women into boxes and endorse specific types of behaviour. As such they are not helpful if you want to engage women.

One big risk is therefore to essentialize women (and men for that matter). There are many differences between women and not all women will have the same priorities. Think of Anna. Anna has just returned from a women's leadership training. She is on a high after this training and really wants to push her career. She makes an appointment with her line manager to discuss how she can advance her career. She is well prepared. She has list of what developmental experiences she seeks and how she wants to hit her targets. All fired up to talk about her career, she sits down with her line manager who asked her 'I remember that you have just attended this leadership programme for women. When do you want to have children then?'. This question threw Anna completely. She was not there to talk about having children at all. In fact she had decided a long time ago that she did not want to have children of her own. She wanted to talk about how to progress her career. Not being prepared for this question, Anna did not know how to respond. She mumbled something but felt so misunderstood that she was not able to recover from this. Her line manager was probably proud of himself that he had remembered the women's leadership training and he clearly thought that this training was to figure out when to have children. He presumed that the women's leadership programme would have clarified those questions for women and that this is what she wanted to talk about now. He probably patted himself on the back for being that understanding. He knew from previous experience that this was something on many women's minds and he wanted to address is right out and thought that this would support the woman. However, it is not hard to image a myriad of reasons why such a question would be ill conceived. For instance just think about how a woman, who underwent many unsuccessful in-vitro fertilization (IVF) cycles might feel to such a comment! Again, the senior leader was well-meaning and wanted to be supportive, but this completely backfired because the question he asked was not only potentially offensive but also not what the woman wanted to talk about – she actually wanted to make herself available for a key assignment and felt empowered after the leadership training to take it on. A key lesson here is not to make the mental leap from one woman to another and presume that all women will want the same thing.

Because women are not a homogenous group and have different life experiences and perspectives, it is not surprising that women do not agree on the best strategies for gender equality. It would be naive to assume that such an agreement would exist if academic research is yet to reach a consensus on what works for gender equality.[7]

Men's resistance

"We are already diverse – we are all different MBTI (Myers Briggs Type Indicator) types!". At a meeting in a pharmaceutical organization, the middle managers voiced strong resistance to being asked to think about how diversity could increase in their business. From the outside the men were rather similar – they were all white, middle class, attended a small set of universities, and worked with the organization for a long time. Yet when they looked around the table, all they saw was difference. As part of a team building exercise they had all done an MBTI and they had heard how they are all different and how to accommodate this difference productively when working together as a team. Having different personality types had left them with the impression that they were diverse already. This was used to claim that they already had a lot of cognitive diversity in the team and any additional efforts to generate diversity would not be beneficial. Why would they need to increase diversity even more?

Such resistance by men is a common feature in organizations. Being already diverse is of course here used as a defence to avoid any change. A version of this argument is that everyone brings a unique set of elements of diversity to work, and this should be valued. Focusing on single categories like gender is reducing the diversity that humans hold and means that their unique diversity is not appreciated. Another common disclaimer of why change is needed is to say that there is already a woman in a senior position. The presence of one woman is used to claim that no further action on gender equality is required.

However, the majority of men seem to resist gender equality efforts because they believe such efforts to be a result of a quota. As mentioned before, having a quota for women is equated with the idea that merit is eroded and that men are now disadvantaged. The core idea is that women get advanced regardless of their actual performance and if a position comes up, women are given preference over men. However, it is not only the contentious issue of a quota that seems to be voiced regularly by men.

"Are you back from your spa break?" With this remark Laura was welcomed back by Lukas after attending a three-day women's leadership development programme. Laura was surprised by this remark – the leadership training was intense and there was certainly no time for spa treatments! However, many men construct events set up for women to develop as leaders as simply a fun trip without any acknowledgement that such trainings can be rather demanding. Carmen, another participant of a women's leadership programme reported that she was asked by a male colleague "where is the men's leadership programme?". Not only are such programmes for women ridiculed, they are also used to claim that women get something 'extra' whereas men are left behind. Initiatives for women to develop as leaders are often either not taken seriously and/or seen as an extra benefit for women which men miss out on.

So how do you deal with such issues when you confront them? One of the CEOs I spoke to during my research had a clear strategy for dealing with such criticism: Tim would call it out. One time a very junior colleague, Mark, simply barged into Tim's office without an appointment to voice his frustration about the gender equality efforts in the organization, particularly the mentoring programme for women. Tim told Mark:

'Listen, you just walk into my office without an appointment. That's a bold move. This is something I never witnessed a woman doing. Neither to complain nor to ask for advice. The fact alone that you felt that you could walk into my office to voice your discontent with a company policy is the exact reason why we need the development programmes for women such as the mentoring programme that you complain about!'

Tim thus addressed Mark's behaviour head on and used his behaviour to show why a mentoring programme for women is needed.

Men often challenge other men for engaging in gender equality. Think for instance of Oliver who had taken on a leading role in the gender equality programme in his organization. When he mentioned this to his colleague Tristan. Tristan remarked "my condolences". This remark was meant to imply that Oliver was clearly not doing this work voluntarily. Tristan seems to imply that Oliver must have been asked to do it and that it was not an enjoyable or rewarding task.

Such incidents of men belittling or even mocking other men for their engagement in gender equality were surprisingly common in my research. How can we explain that? One explanation is homosociality. Homosociality is how hegemonic masculinity, the dominant form of masculinity, is maintained.[8] The word homosociality often creates some confusion because it relates to rather academic language. Homosociality refers to men's non-sexual attraction to other men.[9] This results for instance in that men support other men because they remind them of themselves.[10] Homosociality is also used to show how hegemonic masculinity should be performed and it thus functions as a distinction to those who do not comply with hegemonic masculinity.[11] Displaying homosociality includes men displaying competitiveness and treating women as sexual objects.[12] If men are not performing hegemonic masculinity through homosociality by for instance supporting gender equality they are often ridiculed to show that they are stepping out of line. That is one explanation of why men belittling or mocking other men is so common when men step forward as change makers for gender equality.

How can you respond to such belittlement and mockery? In the example mentioned previously, Oliver responded by asking what Tristan meant by his remark. Oliver explained why he has taken on this work for gender equality. He also elaborated what he gets out of it both in terms of career as well as in terms of personal sense of achievement. Another response would have been to join Tristan and mock the gender equality effort. If Oliver had done this, he would have contributed to undermining gender equality but arguably would have build camaraderie with other men. However, in challenging this assertion and moving it out of the 'humorous remark' zone, Oliver might not have been able to build connection with other men (that is enact homosociality and by extension hegemonic masculinity) but he was able to strengthen the credibility of the gender equality efforts at his organization. And maybe Oliver even encouraged Tristan to reflect on his remark.

Another time I witnessed how Oliver said "Well done, Axel". Axel looked at Oliver slightly irritated as if he was not sure what he is being congratulated on. Oliver said, "I noticed that with your most recent appointment, your team is now 50 per cent men and 50 per cent women. That is excellent news". Axel appeared slightly surprised by this as if he had not fully realized that his team would be gender balanced with another woman joining his team. It clearly had not crossed his mind that the appointment of a woman into his team means that he now manages a team with 50 per cent women and 50 per cent men. By pointing this out, Oliver was raising awareness about the importance of gender equality and how specific activities can achieve it. Although Axel was not resisting gender equality, he clearly did not have it front of mind and Oliver's intervention changed that.

In sum, if you encounter resistance or in fact ignorance by other men on gender equality, you need to fight the corner for gender equality. Sure, it would be easier to avoid this by simply joining those who resist gender equality or are ignorant about it. However, by explaining why gender equality is needed and how it can be achieved, you can actively support gender equality.

Listening

Gert, a senior leader in his organization, is facing budget cuts. He is required to cut 10 per cent of his budget. Looking at the items, he spots a charge for coaching sessions. Trying to find out what these coaching sessions are he discovers that the charge is for coaching some of the women in his team receive. Gert earmarks the charge for the coaching session to be cut. Upon discovering that their coaching sessions have been victim of the budget cuts, three of the women affected make an appointment with Gert to discuss this. Claudia for instance explains that working with the coach has prepared her to lead a big project for Gert. Sandra recounts how the coach was instrumental in her returning from her maternity leave, and Yvette illustrates how her recent promotion was in large parts due to the fact that a coach has worked through application with her. After hearing these stories, Gert leans back and says "I had no idea".

Although we have seen so far that enabling seems to relate to dealing with resistance, in some instances you might not confront any resistance but simply ignorance. For instance, Gert did not realize what a profound impact coaching sessions had for women in his team and how those coaching sessions were instrumental in achieving in developing women and thus achieving gender equality. Gert was unaware of this because he had never worked with a coach let alone listened to the experiences that women who he managed had with coaches. Gert wondered, was it simply a question of not making the time to listen to the experiences of others? Was he not creating spaces where these issues could be discussed? He concluded that time and space certainly played a role, but he had noticed something else in his behaviour. When listening to Claudia, Gert was sceptical about the value of a coach. Surely, Claudia would talk up the experience because she wanted to enjoy more coaching sessions. He bit his tongue and instead of judging listened to Sandra and then Yvette. Only after listening to these three stories, he started to see a pattern on why coaching was very important for the women. He would not have seen that pattern if he only had listened to one of the women.

One of the common complaints about men in organizations chimes with what Gert initially experienced – he simply did not believe the women he spoke with. Very often when women try to share their experiences, this is met with an immediate judgement commonly denying the woman her experience by stating that this is 'just your point of view' or 'that is not my experience'. Of course your experience is going to be different because you are positioned in a different way than other people. This requires men to try and see the world from a different vantage point. Acknowledging perspective is central here. Where you stand will affect what you can see and if you change positions you might be able to notice new things that were hidden from sight before. This means that the only way you can access information about the experience of others is to try and understand their point of view.

The main reaction many men have towards hearing experiences of difference is one of disbelief. "This is not my experience of the organization, so you must be wrong." A gut reaction that many people follow is to deny other people's experience. This can take different forms. First, people might simply state that this experience is not aligned with their own experience of the organization. It implies that their experience of the world is less true than their own. Individuals just need to align their experience with the majority experience and they will be okay. Second, it might be suggested that the person is overly sensitive. A common allegation is that women see everything through a gender lens and that this clouds their judgement. The assumption is here that they need to adjust the frame of reference to ensure that they make the right experiences. Both approaches have in common that they deny people their own experience.

How can that be changed? Active listening is certainly central here. You need to be open to hear others and more importantly to hear others without judgement. It is central for men to cultivate active listening skills if they want to support gender equality. Do not offer judgment. Jumping immediately to a solution to an issue risks implying that the individual who made those experiences is somehow not well adjusted and needs to modify him- or herself to better fit in. There is ample literature on how women can modify themselves to be better leaders already. They probably do not need your advice on what they can do differently.

Resist the urge to evaluate or put their experience into perspective. For instance you might remark that you had not been aware of how this felt because your life experience is different. Do not try to argue with the experience by for example offering an explanation why a person has acted in a specific way. Instead encourage further details. For instance you can ask "how did that make you feel?" or "could you expand on this aspect". Invite others to add more detail to their experience to allow you to get a fuller picture. Offer comments of support such as "I did not realize that this felt like this for you" or "thanks for sharing this with me". Rather than denying that the person had certain emotions acknowledge those emotions by saying "I understand that this must have been very upsetting for you". In some cases it might be appropriate to state that you have not experienced this but that you can understand why it was irritating, upsetting or hurtful.

It is key here to avoid overgeneralized perspectives but instead pay attention to particularities that might only be visible from that person's vantage point. It is not about being right or wrong but about acknowledging that different experiences exist. However, although these experiences are individual, it is useful to reflect on how these experiences relate to wider social structures like sexism or racism that exist in society. These wider social structures create those experiences for individuals. This is important because it avoids blaming the individual for experiences that she or he makes. It is important to call out the wider social structures that lead to those experiences. This avoids the sense of individualization that I discussed earlier. Another really useful way of listening is to ask women what you can do differently. How could you or other men avoid such experiences in the future. This shifts the discussion to a more structural level.

Such conversations require trust on both sides. Women need to trust that the men are listening to them and taking their experience seriously. Men need to trust that these are not personal attacks towards them but rather speak to a wider social phenomenon. If you are able to listen to women without judgement, validate their experiences, see gender as a systematic issue, resist the urge to offer individual solutions and instead try to learn what you and other men can do differently, you have the opportunity of using the experience of putting yourself into the shoes of others to develop your own learning on how you can create gender equality at work. This is not an activity you do once and then you have made the required experiences. Instead it is a continual practice that you need to engage in to learn as much as possible about experiences that are different to your own.

Putting yourself in the shoes of others

In order to act in gender-inclusive ways, it is central that you develop the ability to see the world from a different vantage point. Here are some ideas how you can put yourself in the shoes of others.

1. Listen carefully without judgement.
2. Ensure that you validate rather than challenge experience.
3. Provide affirmation that you heard similar stories from other people.
4. Resist the urge to suggest solutions to a problem.
5. Ask what you and other men can do.

4
MODELLING

Cuthbert was keen on advancing gender equality in his organization. As a senior leader he had a lot of levers at his disposal to achieve this. He paid attention to biases when hiring and also mentored various women. One of the women he was mentoring was Phillipa. Phillipa was a smart and capable woman who he was convinced would go far in the organization. When speaking to Phillipa during one of their mentoring conversations he stressed that she should really find a female role model which she can emulate. He asked her to bring a list to the next meeting so that they can discuss potential role models in detail. Cuthbert was reasonably proud of making such an adept suggestion. Straight afterwards he was talking to Ben, one of the junior men he was mentoring. They discussed how Ben could be a role model for others in the organization and how this would advance his leadership. Reflecting on the two conversations,

Cuthbert was struck by the fact that he had advised a woman to find a role model while he advised a man to be a role mode. He was wondering if there was a gender dimension in the advice he was giving.

Research has in fact shown that in books for aspiring leaders men and women receive rather different advice: men are encouraged to be role models for others while women are encouraged to find a role model.[1] Such gender differences in the advice you might give as an inclusive leader is central for understanding how you can practise what you preach.

Role models for women

In order to support women in his organization better on their journey to leadership, Carlos has decided to read a few books written by well-known women. On his desk were of course *Lean In* by Sheryl Sandberg, *Thrive* by Arianna Huffington and *A Good Time to Be a Girl* by Helena Morrissey. Carlos skim-read most of them. These women all impressive he thought. Yet he also felt slightly intimated by them. They were clearly very successful and had a lot of resources at their disposal. However how realistic was it for the women he worked with to relate to these hyper successful women? He decided to ask some of his colleagues. They confirmed that these women and their stories were inspiring. Yet they also felt that these women were very far removed from their daily activities. The women felt that the advice these women imparted could often not be translated into their own lives.

Women in leadership regularly publish books that combine features of self-help books with autobiographies. These books often differ markedly from book that men in leadership might write. The most notable difference is that gender is something discussed in the books by women but rarely makes an appearance in books written by men. Issues like how to deal with domestic chores, child care, or how to find a life partner are central themes in the books written by women yet rarely feature in the books written by men. Books written by women also speak to largely women as their audience while most books written by men speak to everyone.

When studying the self-help cum autobiography books by women leaders, we found that the advice the books impart normally falls into three areas.[2] The first area is confidence. Confidence is mentioned in such books as a way to overcome any barriers that women might confront. While undoubtedly important, confidence is made out to be a panacea for gender inequality. By simply being more confident women are able to avoid gender inequality. However, confidence also means that it is in the hand of women to make changes. That is certainly empowering. Women are seen as being able to change their own destiny by working on themselves and turning inward. In their excellent book *Confidence Culture* Shani Orgad and Rosalind Gill provide an engaging account of how confidence for women is mobilized today to explain how gender equality can be reduced.[3] They argue that while women might feel empowered, it puts them in charge of changing gender inequality rather than for instance holding organizations to account to create more gender equality.

Returning to the analysis of books for women in leadership, the second theme we found relates to control.[4] Women are encouraged to be in control of all parts of their lives. This includes work, their children, their husbands and themselves. Everything has to be tightly managed and controlled such as having a personal assistant sending a schedule to a husband to compare diaries, and children's household duties. The books also advice that sometimes one has to draw a line and make time for yourself.

The final theme that was present in the books is courage. The books advised women to have courage and persevere in the face of adversity. But most courage seems to come down to sheer hard work. Rather than enjoying shopping or a massage, these books talk about how working hard is the key to success. As such, the responsibility for succeeding or failing is handed over to women themselves. Although this might be inspirational because again it is the individual woman who can secure her success, such perspectives ignore that success is often far more complex than simply being the result of hard work.

So should Carlos advocate that women read these books by celebrity women? These books can certainly provide some inspiration to women but they might equally well be intimidating them. If your life seems remote from the context the books describe, the real-life lessons one can take from the books might be limited. Nevertheless they might provide some inspirations for some women. Contextualizing the advice the books provide would be central for any reading recommendation.

What about getting other men to read those books? The main anticipated audience of the books is clearly women but men might take away some useful insights on how some women become leaders. However, given that remoteness of the context to daily situations the takeaways here might be limited. In sum, it might be more beneficial for Carlos to get women in his team to reflect on closer role models. These could be people they work with or know in their private life. Such closer role models might provide clues on what they admire in others and might want to emulate.

Be a role model

When I shared with Jack that women are encouraged to find a role model while men are encouraged to be one, he wondered in how far this would limit his ability to model gender equality. He was aware of the fact that if he decided to be a role model for gender equality, he might repeat the gender stereotypes attached to this advice. I agreed that this is a valid concern. We discussed that first of all Jack should respond to this by encouraging women to be role models for others: women as well as men. However, that did not resolve Jack's dilemma. We decided to unpack this a bit more. Was it really problematic to be a role model as a man? We agreed that this is not the case. Men like women should be role models for others. However, what is crucial is how they inhabit the role of the role model. If the role model is set up to be a heroic leader that others follow in the traditional sense this would be less desirable. Instead the move is towards a post-heroic role model who models behaviours that would support a post-heroic approach to leadership.

But how would such a post-heroic approach look in practice? Let's explore a few examples of how post-heroic leadership might unfold. The first scenario takes us into a meeting situation. Lina makes a suggestion on how to resolve an issue. However, this contribution is not listened to. Shortly after, Matthias makes the same suggestion and Matthias' suggestion is received as a fantastic idea. What could you do? If you notice such an incident you could for instance amplify Lina's idea when you notice that it does not get any traction. You should clearly attribute the idea to Lina to avoid that the idea is seen as yours. Alternatively, if you notice that Matthias gets the credit for this idea, you could say "This is rather similar to what Lina said before. Should we revisit this idea? Lina, could you please expand on it?". Such micro-inventions ensure that women's contributions are given credit. This is a way to role model behaviour of what gender-inclusive leadership can look like.

Sponsoring women

Paul was asked if he could suggest someone to lead a business-critical project. This project would certainly be a career accelerator for whoever took it on. His mind immediately went to two men who he would trust to advance this project. He had worked with both of them and would feel comfortable to put them forward. However, he then wondered if there might be a woman who he could suggest. He was hesitant to suggest a woman. Would people presume that they have a relationship outside of work? Would the woman do a good job? Would he be willing to put his reputation on the line for the woman he had in mind?

Such questions are rather common. They result in that women are less often sponsored than men. But what is sponsorship? You might be familiar with mentoring. A mentor is someone who is often assigned to give you advice on how to develop your career. They might share details about the organizational culture or how to navigate a tricky situation. That is useful but research has shown that women are in fact over mentored – they get a lot of advice.[5] But women do not get as much sponsorship as men.[6] Sponsorship is something that is earned rather than assigned. A sponsor fights your corner if you are not in the room. A sponsor is willing to put his or her reputation on the line for you. Like Paul in the previous example, many men have no problem in opening career opportunities for other men. In fact, this is part and parcel of how homosociality, men's non-sexual attraction to other men[7], works. Yet men supporting women breaks homosociality but also often leads to a lot of speculation such as about a romantic involvement. Men are hesitant to put their reputation on the line for a woman. They might be uncertain if the woman would be able to handle the pressure of leading a business-critical project or they might be concerned about what others might think about it.

Paul eventually decided to put Evelyn forward. However, before suggesting her, Paul and Evelyn have a conversation about it. Evelyn is concerned. The business-critical project sounds very much like a glass cliff, she said. The glass cliff is a phenomenon where women are appointed to leadership roles during a crisis when risk of failure is highest.[8] A commonly cited example is Theresa May becoming prime minister after the UK had decided to leave the EU (also known as Brexit). Or if organizations perform poorly financially they are more likely to appoint a woman in a leadership role. While some research has confirmed the glass cliff, other research has not found any evidence of its existence.[9] Regardless or not of whether the glass cliff as a phenomenon exists, it is important to keep the possibility that a position might be a glass cliff in mind. Women are often advised to do their research and check for instance the financial health of the company or who on the board of directors could support them. However, it also seems that if women have the opportunity to rise into leadership it is often due to the fact that no one else wants this leadership role because risk of failure is high.

Paul acknowledged to Evelyn that there is a risk in taking up the role because the project might fail. Evelyn then asks if she simply should turn it down given the fact that it is a risk for her career. Paul reflects on this, but responds that he thinks she should give it a go. There might simply be not another opportunity for such a business-critical project in the near future. And if so, she might not get it. Paul asks what he could do to support her. They work out a plan how Paul and other colleagues can provide support by for instance acknowledging that the project is challenging and might fail regardless of who takes it on. However, more importantly Paul suggests exit strategies. If the project is not going well, he shares how Evelyn might hand over responsibility without it looking like failure. He also wants Evelyn to make a list of what she can learn from such an assignment and to measure her success based on this list rather than on the success of the overall project.

Paul thus created an environment where Evelyn could do well. He and others will support her. She knows what she wants to take away from the project and she is clear on how to exit if needs be. Rather than presuming that because it might be a glass cliff, women should not take on a role, they might require a safety net in case they fall off the glass cliff.

Sponsorship means to support someone if he or she is not in the room. While men as change agents for gender equality can sponsor, for women it is important to keep in mind that sponsorship in itself might be a necessary but not sufficient condition. You also need to be ready to support the person you sponsor. This entails giving general advice like a mentor, but it also means to ensure the success of the woman you sponsor by creating an environment where this is possible.

Mansplaining

I am sitting at a dinner with other members of faculty who have recently joined the university. The topic comes to gender equality. I mention to the person next to me, Wole, that there has been a lot of change in universities in regard to awareness for gender equality. Wole, not knowing my area of expertise, disagrees. He argued that gender inequality is as pronounced as ever in universities and that I should just talk to his female colleagues. I felt slightly amused by this because I have spent about 20 years of my life researching gender equality in different settings, yet I am 'schooled' by a colleague who is clearly unaware of my research interests. What Wole was doing was a good thing. He tried to support gender equality by telling me that gender inequality is still happening. However, what he ended up doing is unknowingly explaining my research topic to me.

Such experiences are rather common and countless colleagues who focus on gender equality regularly report being 'mansplained' their research topic. Mansplaining is defined as a man explaining something to a woman in a patronizing fashion that she likely already knows. It is regularly called out as a practice that perpetuates gender equality. So, in the previous example, Wole by explaining my research topic to me was effectively perpetuating gender inequality by mansplaining.

Wole tried to do the right thing for gender equality; he was trying to point out that gender inequality still exists and to avoid that people construct their workplaces as gender neural. Coincidentally, this was an important topic in my earlier research, where I have documented how individuals work very hard to construct their workplaces as gender neutral.[10] I have termed this gender fatigue.[11] Women in particular notice gender inequality in their immediate context yet deny that gender inequality matters for them. What was fascinating is that women denied the relevance of gender in their working lives in spite of evidence of the contrast. The same interviewee who had talked about gender being not relevant just before, would then recount a sexist event that she struggled with. In this research I suggested that women and men want to live in a world where gender does not matter.[12] They have the belief that everyone can be successful regardless of background. While this is certainly a desirable ideal, the everyday work experiences will still be littered with gender. What individuals thus do is to work hard to ignore those experiences where gender plays a role to pretend that gender equality has been achieved. Any evidence to the contrary is ignored. Pretending that gender does not matter is therefore a defence mechanism that individuals employ to get through their day and come to work the following day.

Although we have previously suggested that men who deny women's experiences need to develop listening skills, men should resist the urge to explain women's experiences to them. This risks appearing as mansplaining. We have discussed earlier that it is natural for us to presume that everyone sees the world just like we do. The reality seems to have an objective quality and it is common to assume that how I experience the world is how other people experience the world, too. However, the experiences we make and how we make sense of those experiences, are individual processes. A woman of colour is going to make different experiences to a white man every day and this past experience will guide her in how to make sense of new experiences. If this woman is not listened to in a meeting she might decide not to speak up next time and will not be able to make a meaningful contribution. The different experiences we make will sum up over time and we develop filters to see read our experience through those filters. In this context, it is less helpful to try and explain the experience that women make to them.

The risk of mansplaining is a serious one for men who want to be change makers for gender equality. They have invested time and resources to learn about gender equality and want to speak about this topic. This in itself is a good thing. However, you have to be attuned to how you bring gender into the discussion. Do not claim that you have some superior knowledge to women and do not try to explain women's experiences to them. Instead go back to the listening mode discussed in the 'visioning' chapter. Try and understand why a woman has different experiences by asking questions and listening. Resist the urge to share your knowledge on gender equality in a patronizing way and instead listen to women on why they have these experiences.

Calling out

"Let's pause right here." Eddy was in a hiring committee with his boss Jason. Jason was very keen to hire the male candidate, Jackson. Jackson had gone to the same university as Jason. Jackson reminded Jason a lot of himself when he was younger. The female candidate Cassandra was on paper as good as Jackson, but Jason felt that something was 'off' with her. She did not appear as assertive as Jackson. As Eddy could sense that his boss Jason was keen on getting Jackson in, Eddy pressed pause on the conversation. He said that while Jackson was impressive, Eddy was not sure that he had what it takes to lead the organization forward. Five years ago he might have been the right leader but in today's environment he is less likely to be the best candidate required to navigate the challenges ahead. He agreed that Cassandra came across as less assertive. However, he remarked that if Cassandra as a woman from Indian descent would be as assertive as Jackson that would be read as unusual if not aggressive.

What Eddy does in this discussion about candidates is what is often termed 'calling out'. Calling out refers to calling out biases and inequalities that might exist in the evaluation of others. Job interviews are arenas where gender inequalities often manifest. There are three effects that I have observed in particular in regard to job interviews. The first is similarity attraction. We are more comfortable with people like ourselves and would ideally hire clones of ourselves. Homosociality, as discussed before, is a similar concept but similarity attraction is a slightly more encompassing term. This similarity can be expressed for instance in regard to having the same hobbies (golfing is often cited) or having gone to the same university (regularly elite universities). We often also see ourselves in the candidates we interview. They might remind us of ourselves as their age. All of those things create a bond between the interviewer and the interviewee. Eddy draws attention to this behaviour in the previous example.

A second dynamic is that there is a tendency for us to replace the norm. We are more likely to pick people who 'fit in'. Fitting in often means that they resemble the majority of individuals, particularly successful ones, in the organization. We tend to recruit individuals who fit the same mould, and this gives us the illusion that they are fitting in. However, all we are doing is to replace the norm – we are recruiting people who are more similar to the majority of people.

The third dynamic is that we use different yardsticks to evaluate men and women. A woman who is displaying the same assertiveness as a man might be judged negatively. If the woman is showing a behaviour that is less commonly expected in women, we react to this dissonance between expected and actual behaviour by judging a person negatively.

If you see such instances in job interviews or beyond a useful strategy might be to call it out. While calling it out is often equated with a direct challenge to the person, this might not be the best way to proceed. In such cases a sense for diplomacy might be key. In the example already mentionned, while Eddy felt confident to address these dynamics with his boss, in many situations his boss might have felt threatened and told off which is unlikely to change behaviour. Instead it might lead to aggression. For example if you notice that a woman is cut off in a meeting situation by the same person, in some situations it can be helpful to address this in the meeting. You might say that you notice that your colleague has not finished her point. However, in other situations that might be highly disruptive, and you might chose instead to address this with a colleague in private conversation outside of the meeting. Again, depending on the colleague saying that "you cut off a female colleague" might not be the way to go but maybe saying that your female colleague has a lot to say on this topic might be enough to correct this behaviour.

Calling out is a central activity for a change maker but the calling out does not have to be confrontational. In fact, in many instances, more subtle interventions are highly effective. Yet, in other situations where gender bias is deeply engrained and does not change with subtle nudges, a more direct approach to calling out bias is required. Even if an intervention has worked before, it might not work again. A leader who wants to be a change maker for gender equality needs the sensitivity to decide which approach might be best suited in a given situation.

Double standards

Pierre had to move a Zoom meeting with his boss William. He was hesitant how to phrase this. In the end he decided to be frank, and he wrote to William in an email that, if possible, he would like to move the meeting. Pierre explained that he has to take care of his children because day care is closed due to COVID-19. William appreciated the openness and was happy to rearrange the Zoom meeting. In fact he saw what Pierre did as an ideal example of how men can make their caring responsibilities more visible. William decided to mention this during the next team meeting leading to some very appreciative comments. However, after the meeting Irene approached William. She mentioned that she appreciated that William praised Pierre's caring responsibilities. However, she, too, had to juggle work and family during COVID-19 but she did not get a mention. In fact, she had the feeling that others resented her for it and presumed that she did not take her job seriously. William realized that inadvertently he had contributed to a gendered double standard.

Double standards are a persistent theme in regard to gender in the workplace. Men and women are often judged by different yardsticks without people realizing it. The example cited previously is a fairly typical one. Men are praised for being active fathers who care for their children but if women are active mothers this is often regarded as a negative for their career. We also saw a similar dynamic in regard to the hiring decision discussed earlier in regard to assertiveness.

The same skills and behaviours are perceived and evaluated differently depending on who is performing them. In the research I conducted for my PhD I found a striking example of such a dynamic.[13] In the early

2000s there was a big focus on bringing more women into programming work. Like today, women were underrepresented among the rows of programmers. At the same time programming was increasingly perceived as a social activity. Rather than following the idea that lone hackers are coding on their own, software programming was seen as a collaborative endeavour and required not only programmers to work to together but to also service a client need. As such, social and emotional skills took centre stage. Given the fact that women are often presumed to have social and emotional skills, it is not hard to imagine which arguments were made to support the idea that more women should join programming work: women bring exactly the social and emotional skills that programming work needs and as such more women should be recruited. However, it is also well documented that if women display social and emotional skills that is rarely valued as extraordinary.[14] I showed in my work on programmers that it is in fact not women who profit from displaying social and emotional skills but men.[15] As men are presumed not be good with social and emotional skills they were rewarded for displaying such skills. However, when women displayed those skills, they were seen as what women do anyway and not requiring any special recognition.

Such differences in how skills are evaluated in people have strong repercussions for who is hired and promoted. We have mentioned earlier that women who are assertive are often seen as aggressive and that this can affect if they are seen as a good hire. We see similar effects in regard to careers in general. The glass ceiling metaphor is familiar to most people, and we have encountered it before. As a reminder, it describes how women can see the higher echelons of organizations but cannot get to them; an invisible barrier holds them back. Much has been written about the utility of using the glass ceiling as a metaphor for women in the workplace and most notably it has been suggested that a more apt metaphor of women in leadership is that of a labyrinth.[16] Rather than having a glass ceiling that one has to shatter once and for all, women in leadership are often in a labyrinth with many dead ends and turns which makes their leadership experience more challenging.

Although the glass ceiling is commonly referenced, a less known metaphor to describe gender at work is that of the glass escalator. It is often suggested that the glass ceiling is really the outcome of women being in a minority position. Women are different from the norm that dominates leadership in organizations and this minority position might affect women's experiences. However, women are not in a minority in all areas of work. Think for instance of primary school teaching or nursing where women form the majority. Is a glass ceiling existing in those professions for men? Research has looked into this matter and has discovered that a glass ceiling does not exist for men in female-dominated professions.[17] Instead of confronting a glass ceiling, men can ride the glass escalator; that is men are more likely to be promoted. If men work in female-dominated professions, they are in a minority, but the effects of their minority status are positive. Since men working in female-dominated professions are seen as unusual, they are often promoted to be in leadership positions. As such, their careers accelerate ahead of those women working in these professions. It should be noted that these effects only hold true for white men.

The gendered double standard is deep seated and goes back to how we expect men and women in society to be and behave. We expect women to be socially competent and as such do not reward them for showing those skills. Men are not expected to be socially competent, yet if they show this competence they are rewarded. We expect women to be caring for their families, yet if men do the same, it deserves praise. Women are in the minority in leadership positions which contributes to the glass ceiling but if men are in a minority position in female-dominated professions they can enjoy faster career development by riding the glass escalator.

For a change maker for gender equality, understanding the deep-seated nature of such double standards is central. But how can you resolve this double standard? Due to the fact that these double standards are intertwined with how gender is understood in modern societies, it is not possible to resolve this double standard completely. However, you can raise awareness for this. As such, there is nothing wrong with William celebrating Pierre's role as an active father and that needs to happen to show that it is not just women who have caring responsibilities. At the same, time William might have signalled that he is aware that the similar situation for women would be read differently. That could have been used as a point of reflection for the team. Over time double standards might reduce but in the meantime change makers for gender equality have to be aware that these double standards exist and how to tackle them proactively.

Walking the talk

Being a role model for gender-inclusive leadership is challenging because gender is full of double standards. The following questions might help on your journey:

1. If asked to suggest role models for women, find novel and unexpected role models that break the mould.
2. Instead of lecturing women, ask them about their expertise on different issues.
3. Proactively advocate for women to advance their careers when they are not in the room.
4. If you are unsure if you encountered a gender double standard, ask yourself if saying the same thing about a woman/man would have a different meaning.
5. Have a repertoire of useful interventions at your disposal if you see exclusionary behaviour.

5
FORGING YOUR PATH AS A CHANGE MAKER

In the previous three chapters, we have seen how visioning, enabling and modelling are important steps on the path towards inclusive leadership. In this final chapter, we will bring the different aspects of the path of inclusive leadership for men together.

Authentic leadership for gender equality

"Well, I learned that I am biased and now I know why" one man said to which another man responded "At least we have confirmation now" and a third man observed "Complete waste of my time". I am sitting in front of a room where an unconscious bias awareness training in a bank has just taken place and based on the conversation I overheard, I am not sure that those men gained much from this training.

Men are often not explicitly addressed when it comes to changing efforts in regard to gender equality. Sure they might be implicit recipients of unconscious bias awareness training, which is often used as an attempt to debias decision making processes. Gender equality is traditionally conceptualized as women's work. The presumption is that women have most to gain from gender equality and it is thus in their interest to make it happen. It is therefore not surprising that we see an abundance of self-help books that aim at telling women how they can shape their work and life to make it to the top. Similarly most initiatives for gender equality, diversity and inclusion are led by those who seen as different from the majority such as women.

An attempt to speak directly to men comes via the construction of men as champions of or allies for gender equality. They are also often called 'male feminists'. The addition of 'male' to 'feminist' suggests that feminists are by definition women. Like with the addition of 'male' to 'nurse', it is signalled that the gender of the person is not what one would expect. While the language to address men in change towards gender equality remains problematic and often appeals to traditional ideas of heroes who rescue the damsel-in-distress, it also speaks to the importance of engaging men in gender equality work in organizations. Providing some concrete tools on how this can be achieved is likely to prove more efficient than an unconscious bias awareness training.

But what can men actually do? The answer this book has offered is the path of the change maker. Men who want to take action on gender equality first need to develop a vision that allows them to find their voice on gender equality. Why are they supporting gender equality? How do they see their change potential? How can they move beyond styling themselves as heroes? The second step is enabling. This means starting to understand where resistance towards gender equality might come from and how it can be addressed by for instance listening. The third step is about modelling. This includes thinking about what advice you give women, who role models for women could be, how you can sponsor women and call out double standards that exist around gender equality.

If you picked up this book, the likelihood is that you want to become a more gender-inclusive leader. Regardless of where you are on the path to becoming a more gender-inclusive leader, this book has provided you with some ways in which you can refine your actions. The path of the change maker provides a range of tools in your toolkit that can be used flexibility in a variety of settings and contexts. There are probably many more practices that might be relevant in your context, which I have not addressed explicitly in this book. This is due to the fact that your path of becoming a change maker for gender equality will be dependent on what feels right for you. It asks you to reflect critically on what type of leader for gender equality you want to be and what concrete actions support that. There is no one-size-fits-all approach, and it is down to your own capacity to critically reflect on your positions and actions. While this might appear as more work in the short time – it most certainly is – it allows you to develop change agency that is right for you rather than just following a template. Such an approach is unlikely to yield authentic results.

This book encourages you to experiment with an approach that works for you in your context. It also means that you need to have openness for not getting it right. As an aspiring change maker for gender equality you will make mistakes. People will take issue with how you engage your change leadership. You will encounter unforeseen obstacles. At times this might be irritating, frustrating and infuriating. In those moments it will be useful to take a step back, take stock, get feedback and try to learn from what has gone wrong and how you could make it better next time round. The path of the change maker is after all a learning process.

The new approach to leadership that will emerge from such efforts is a truly post-heroic one. It is one that allows for constant learning and for not having all the answers. This post-heroic leadership is also one that allows for vulnerability,[1] which represents a drastic departure from how leadership has been thought about in the past. Such an approach to leadership does take courage to do things differently.

Getting things wrong is likely to happen because there are no simple answers in regard to gender equality. If you are promised quick fixes, the likelihood that these fixes will fail is high. Be wary of people promising simply solutions for gender equality. Gender is complex and simplistic understandings of gender are easily debunked by looking at the multitude of academic research that exists on gender. There is no consensus, and many studies find different things. As such simply going with one finding is likely to result in disappointment. Be wary of common-sense explanations around gender. For instance, it is often suggested that women and men are essentially different and that women have unique skills they bring to work. Such thinking is an example of essentialism and seeing men and women as fixed entities. Such an understanding is not only out of sync with current academic research on the subject but also reintroduces the same gender stereotypes that have for long constrained men and women. It can thus be questioned in how far they have much utility at all when changing gender relations. Academic research has time and time again shown that gender is complex and as such dealing with change in regard to gender equality is also complex.

However, change in regard to gender equality is certainly possible. The question is just what the time horizon for change is. Yes, some issues will qualify to be 'low hanging fruit' – you can tackle them to get success fairly quickly. Other issues will not be resolved in the foreseeable future and will require constant attention. As a change maker for gender equality, you need to be able to differentiate between those things you can change quickly and those things that might not be changeable in the next two decades or longer. You need to be able to find strategies to deal with both extremes and everything in between.

In most cases you will continue to work within established organizational boundaries. Rather than introducing radical change from the outside, you will be a change maker working on the inside of organizations. This has been called tempered radicals. Tempered radicals are radical in that they aim to change practices but also tempered in that they do that within organizational settings.[2] Making organizations more gender equal requires the energy of tempered radicals but it also invites us to explore which parts of organizations are no longer functional.

Most organizations have been set up by men and with men in mind. The ideal worker and the ideal leader is imagined to be a man.[3] Fitting women into such systems will likely not succeed and requires much deeper changes in how work is organized and managed than is commonly anticipated. This of course leaves room to look at alternative forms of organizing to see in how far these lead to more or less gender equality. For instance approaches like holacracy offer a different way of organizing[4] but if they will lead to more or less gender equality has not been researched yet.

Most of this book focused on paid work in traditional organizational settings. In research terms this is often called the public sphere as opposed to the private sphere. The private sphere of course holds many levers to create gender equality. We have seen glimpses of that in regard to men who are fathers and how that affects working practices. However, what we have not looked at are the arrangements of gender in the private sphere such as who is doing the grocery shopping, who cares for elderly relatives, who writes the 'thank you notes' and how do those arrangements vary between traditional nuclear families, same-sex families or single parents. These questions are important and change makers need to reflect on how these multitudes of arrangements might interface with paid work.

What is gender-inclusive leadership?

Jerry had heard a lot about diversity and inclusion and had a rough idea what the organization does in regard to diversity and inclusion. However, he was less clear what this actually meant. Jerry thus asked for a meeting with the diversity and inclusion professional in his organization to query how diversity and inclusion is actually defined. Melanie, the diversity and inclusion lead, said that "diversity means being invited to the party, inclusion is being asked to dance".[5] Although the dance metaphor is problematic from a gender perspective because one could argue that it recurs to traditional gender norms where a woman is asked to dance, it is useful to illustrate the difference between diversity and inclusion.

In order to define gender-inclusive leadership, let's take a closer look at the definition of inclusion. Inclusion differs from diversity. Diversity describes the composition of groups or workforces based on observable and non-observable characteristics such as race, ethnicity, gender, class, dis/abilities, sexualities, gender identities, cognitive differences and so on.[6] Diversity focuses on bringing different types of people into the workforce and promoting them. However, bringing people into organizations does not tell you anything about exclusion and inclusion. If you have people in a team who differ from one another, but power is held by one specific group and other individuals are ignored, the ability to profit from diversity is limited. Such dynamics refer to exclusion. Inclusion in contrast means that people can do their job well because they have the required resources and information and have the ability to influence decisions in the organization.[7] In other words inclusion thus focuses on the 'degree to which individuals feel a part of critical organizational processes'.[8] While diversity means bringing in and advancing people that are different from the majority, inclusion means that those individuals are able to contribute fully to the functioning of the organization.

But how can we define gender-inclusive leadership? Throughout the book we have seen a multitude of practices and examples of how gender-inclusive leadership might look and these observations provide clues how gender-inclusive leadership can look. In research terms we have defined gender inclusion inductively through real-life material. We have now a more formal definition of inclusion which can allow us to deductively define gender inclusion. Gender equality is about bringing women and men into the organization and gender inclusion means that women and men are able to have access to the resources and information to fulfil their role in the organization and to influence decision making. The role of the change maker for gender inclusion is then to create an enabling environment where women and men have access to key information and resources and can fully contribute to decision making.

The book purposefully did not start with this definition but instead developed it through the material. The definition is useful at this stage because it solidifies our knowledge in this space. However, if we had started with it, it might have ended up being a theoretical definition without much resonance. By first going through the change-maker framework with a range of practices attached, we can see how this theoretical concept can be filled with actions.

As this book has illustrated, the path of the change maker for gender equality is in many cases not a straightforward one. In fact, it has many bends and turns. You might encounter roadblocks in form of resistance or have to turn around at a dead end. In some cases you will make good progress but in others progress might be painfully slow. In many cases there might not even be a path for you that you can follow, and you have to create this path for yourself. The path of the change maker requires resilience, perseverance and creativity. As such, it is important to keep the purpose of this journey in mind to achieve gender-inclusive leadership. This purpose requires you to keep your energy and motivation up which will not be easy in the busyness of everyday working life. However, by pausing this busyness sporadically to take a quick moment to think about where you are on your journey, you are not only able to reflect on the 'small failures' that need improvement, but you can also celebrate the 'small wins'[9] on your journey.

Five key takeaways

In order to help you on your path as a change maker for gender equality, here are some key takeaways from this book.

1. Men are particularly effective as change agents for gender equality and thus have the responsibility to take others with them on the journey of gender equality.
2. As a man who is a change agent for gender equality, you need to explain why you support gender equality. This means that you need to have a few compelling stories at your disposal which you can use to communicate your vision for how gender equality looks.
3. Your role as a man being a change agent for gender equality means that you need to enable others to follow your path to gender equality. Pay particular attention to resistance and develop a plan to deal with this resistance.
4. You will also have to role model what gender-inclusive leadership looks like. This includes sponsoring women and calling out biases.
5. The path of the change maker for gender-inclusion might have some surprises in stock for you. Be prepared for some twists and turns along the way. Some change will be swift, but other change will take more time and patience.

Good luck on your path!

NOTES

Preface

[1] The report and the comic strips are available under https://www.drop box.com/s/2w39jg263ndo6mh/Linchpin.pdf?dl=0

[2] Kelan (2022).

Chapter 1

[1] OED (2002).

[2] The title echoes Kanter's (1977) seminal book title.

[3] In 1,677 major listed companies across 20 major economies in 2022, 5 per cent of CEOs were women (BoardEx/Altara, 2022).

[4] While the motherhood wage penalty affects all women (Benard and Correll, 2010; Budig and Hodges, 2010), it is particularly expressed in low-wage women (Budig and Hodges, 2010).

[5] Kelan (2014); Wajcman (1998).

[6] The labyrinth of leadership (Eagly and Carli, 2007) is discussed more fully later on.

[7] An excellent discussion of the gender binary systems can be found in Cordelia Fine's (2010) work.

[8] Gratton, Kelan and Walker (2007).

[9] Connell (2020) has provided the leading analysis of hegemonic masculinity. More recently academic discussions have moved to newer conceptions of masculinity (O'Neill, 2015; Anderson and McCormack, 2016; Schwiter, Nentwich and Keller, 2021), which however lie beyond the scope of this book.

[10] Hodges and Budig (2010).

[11] Kelland, Lewis and Fisher (2022).

[12] de Vries (2015); Hekman et al (2017); Kirton, Robertson and Avdelidou-Fischer (2016).

13   Kirsch (2022).
14   Kelan (2022).
15   Brown and Kelan (2020).
16   Cockburn (1991).
17   Martin (2001).
18   Beck and Beck-Gernsheim (2002); Lash (2002).
19   Connell (2020).
20   Kelan and Wratil (2014).
21   The model is commonly attributed to Lewin (1947). However, it has been shown that the change model only took shape after Lewin's death (Cummings, Bridgman and Brown, 2016).
22   Kanter's (1984) classical work on change is useful in this context.
23   Snakes and Ladders is a board game which is also called Chutes and Ladders. If you end up on a ladder you move up in the board game and if you end up on a snake or chute you have to go back.

Chapter 2

1   Brown and Kelan (2020).
2   Gratton et al (2007).
3   Kelan (2020).
4   Dobbin and Kalev (2016).
5   Brown and Kelan (2020).
6   Kelan (2022).
7   Fletcher (2004).
8   Borgatta, Bales and Couch (1954); Organ (1996).
9   MacInnes (1998).
10   Connell (2020).
11   Elliott (2016).
12   Fine (2010); Paoletti (2012).
13   Palacios-Huerta (2022).
14   Kelan (2018).
15   Fletcher (2004).
16   Borrell-Porta, Costa-Font and Philipp (2019).
17   Goffee and Jones (2006).
18   There is a rich body of research on authentic leadership (Sparrowe, 2005; Avolio and Gardner, 2005) but particularly Ibarra's (2015) work is useful for understanding authentic leadership in practice.
19   Denning (2004).

Chapter 3

[1] The leaky pipeline has originally been used for women in science, technology, engineering and mathematics (STEM) (Blickenstaff, 2005) and is now used more widely to describe the low number of women in leadership.
[2] Gill, Kelan and Scharff (2017).
[3] Gill, Kelan and Scharff (2017).
[4] Adamson and Kelan (2019).
[5] Orgad and Gill (2021).
[6] Humbert, Kelan and van den Brink (2019).
[7] Bohnet (2016); Kalev, Dobbin and Kelly (2006).
[8] Bird (1996) and Connell (2020) are useful sources to learn more about homosociality and hegemonic masculinity.
[9] Bird (1996).
[10] Kelan (2015).
[11] Bird (1996).
[12] Bird (1996).

Chapter 4

[1] Ferry and Guthey (2020).
[2] Adamson and Kelan (2019).
[3] Orgad and Gill (2021).
[4] Adamson and Kelan (2019).
[5] Ibarra, Carter and Silva (2010).
[6] Ibarra, Carter and Silva (2010).
[7] Bird (1996).
[8] Ryan and Haslam (2005).
[9] Ryan et al (2016); Main and Gregory-Smith (2018); Bechtoldt, Bannier and Rock (2019).
[10] Kelan and Dunkley Jones (2010).
[11] Kelan (2009b).
[12] Kelan (2009b).
[13] Kelan (2009a).
[14] Phillips and Taylor (1980); Fletcher (1999).
[15] Kelan (2009a).
[16] Eagly and Carli (2007).
[17] Williams (1992).

Chapter 5

[1]   Brown (2012).
[2]   Meyerson and Scully (1995); Kelan and Wratil (2018).
[3]   Schein and Davidson (1993); Schein (2001); Sczesny (2003).
[4]   Robertson (2015).
[5]   I have heard many diversity and inclusion consultants use this expression and it can also found in this article (Hills, 2020).
[6]   Roberson (2006).
[7]   Roberson (2006).
[8]   Roberson (2006, p 215).
[9]   Weick (1984).

ACKNOWLEDGEMENTS

I still remember the time I had the idea to research men's role in gender equality at work. While attending a conference in Istanbul, the hotel room had the most amazing view over the Bosporus. I glanced over Istanbul and contemplated why there is so little academic research on men as change agents for gender equality. My practitioner colleagues regularly stressed the importance of men particularly in senior leadership as change agents, yet academic research on that topic seemed hard to come by. This was in July 2011. As I write this acknowledgement, it is July 2022 – exactly 11 years later. Academic research does certainly take time.

In between July 2011 and July 2022 lies an intensive period of research and engagement on men as change agents. I started out by researching CEOs. I wanted to find out what they do for gender equality. I am very grateful for the support by the Women's Empowerment Principles – Equality Means Business (WEPs), a joint initiative of UN Women and the UN Global Compact. Particularly Ursula Wynhoven, Lauren Gula and

Joan Libby-Hawk were instrumental in making the research happen. The transcription of the interviews was supported by the Department of Management Innovation Fund at King's College London. The results of the CEO study were published with KPMG and I thank Sarah Bond, Melanie Richards and Simon Collins for supporting this project and taking the resulting report to the World Economic Form.

Further details on the CEO report including details on the methodology used and the industries covered can be found in a report:

Kelan, E. and Wratil, P. (2014) *Winning Hearts and Minds: How CEOs Talk About Gender Parity*, KPMG and King's College London. Available Under https://www.dropbox.com/s/a7bagocvmnysa0k/ Hearts%20and%20Minds.pdf?dl=0 [accessed 20 March 2023].

and in two peer reviewed articles:

Kelan, E.K. and Wratil, P. (2018) Post-heroic leadership, tempered radicalism and senior leaders as change agents for gender equality, *European Management Review*, 15(1): 5–18.

Kelan, E.K. and Wratil, P. (2021) CEOs as agents of change and continuity, *Equality, Diversity and Inclusion: An International Journal*, 40(5): 493–509.

Based on the findings from the CEO study, I identified that men as middle managers are understudied yet central for gender equality. I thus applied for a British Academy Mid-Career Fellowship and was extremely fortunate to be selected for this fellowship. I am grateful to the British Academy for supporting the underlying research on middle managers [grant number MD130085].

The report for this project includes comic strips of some of the situations I observed. The report can be found under:

Kelan, E. (2015) Linchpin – Men, Middle Management and Gender Inclusive Leadership, British Academy and Cranfield School of Management. Available Under https://www.dropbox.com/s/2w39jg263ndo 6mh/Linchpin.pdf?dl=0 [accessed 17 March 2023].

The report as well as the following publications provide further details about the methodologies used and the wider results:

Kelan, E.K. (2018) Men doing and undoing gender at work: a review and research agenda, *International Journal of Management Reviews*, 20(2): 544–558.

Kelan, E.K. (2018) Contested terrain: vying for hegemony over gender equality, Lewis, P., Benschop, Y. and Simpson, R. (eds), in *Postfeminism and Organization*, New York: Routledge, pp 105–123.

Kelan, E.K. (2018) Credit where credit is due, de Janasz, S.C. and Crossman, J. (eds), in *Teaching Human Resource Management – An Experiential Approach*, Cheltenham: Edgar Elgar, pp 38–39.

Kelan, E.K. (2020) The inclusive leader, the smart strategist and the forced altruist: subject positions for men as gender equality partners, *European Management Review*, 17(3): 603–613.

Kelan, E.K. (2022) Men as middle managers doing and undoing gender in organizations, *European Management Review*, 19(2): 236–247.

For the CEO and middle manager projects Patricia Wratil was the most amazing research assistant I could have hoped for. Her attention to detail and critical analysis skills were invaluable for both projects. Thank you!

Much of this material was refined and reworked through countless executive education encounters. I would like to thank the participants of those executive education courses for their willingness to engage with the material. I also would like to acknowledge the many discussions I had with academic and practitioner colleagues about this research and the anonymous feedback I had on an earlier draft of this book. Your critical engagement with the findings helped to reshape and reframe them.

I would also like to thank the colleagues in the writing with artificial intelligence workshop at the *Informatica Feminale* in Freiburg in 2022 who used human and artificial intelligence to come up with creative ideas for the title of this book.

All names in the book are pseudonyms, direct quotations are paraphrased, and the details of the observed situations suitably disguised to protect the anonymity of those who shared their experiences with me.

While writing the final drafts of this book, I was fortunate enough to be a Leverhulme Trust Major Research Fellow [grant number MRF-2019–069] focusing most of my time on a rather different topic: the future of work, gender and digitalization.

I would also like to thank the excellent team at Bristol University Press for their support seeing the book through to completion. Paul Stevens, my editor at Bristol University Press, was instrumental in making this book happen. Thanks to Paul for his creativity and courage to develop a format for the book that varies from traditional books as well as for his critical input through the process.

The book would not have been possible without those individuals who agreed to be interviewed and job shadowed for the research. I am immensely grateful for your openness to engage in the research and to critically reflect on your own practices. Without you this research would not have been possible.

REFERENCES

Adamson, M. and Kelan, E.K. (2019) 'Female heroes': celebrity executives as postfeminist role models, *British Journal of Management*, 30(4): 981–996.

Anderson, E. and McCormack, M. (2016) Inclusive masculinity theory: overview, reflection and refinement, *Journal of Gender Studies*, 27(5): 1–15.

Avolio, B.J. and Gardner, W.L. (2005) Authentic leadership development: getting to the root of positive forms of leadership, *The Leadership Quarterly*, 16: 315–338.

Bechtoldt, M.N., Bannier, C.E. and Rock, B. (2019) The glass cliff myth? Evidence from Germany and the UK, *The Leadership Quarterly*, 30(3): 273–297.

Beck, U. and Beck-Gernsheim, E. (2002) *Individualization: Institutionalized Individualism and its Social and Political Consequences*, London: Sage.

Benard, S. and Correll, S.J. (2010) Normative discrimination and the motherhood penalty, *Gender & Society*, 24(5): 616–646.

Bird, S.R. (1996) Welcome to the men's club: homosociality and the maintenance of hegemonic masculinity, *Gender & Society*, 10(2): 120–132.

Blickenstaff, J.C. (2005) Women and science careers: leaky pipeline or gender filter, *Gender and Education*, 17(4): 369–386.

BoardEx/Altara (2022) Global Gender Diversity 2022. Available Under https://altrata.com/reports/global-gen der-diversity-2022 [retrieved 17 March 2023].

Bohnet, I. (2016) *What Works*, Cambridge (MA): Harvard University Press.

Borgatta, E.F., Bales, R.F. and Couch, A.S. (1954) Some findings relevant to the great man theory of leadership, *American Sociological Review*, 19(6): 755–759.

Borrell-Porta, M., Costa-Font, J. and Philipp, J. (2019) The 'mighty girl' effect: does parenting daughters alter attitudes towards gender norms, *Oxford Economic Papers*, 71(1): 25–46.

Brown, B. (2012) *The Power of Vulnerability - Teachings of Authenticity, Connection, and Courage*, Louisville (Colorado): Sounds True.

Brown, S. and Kelan, E. (2020) *Gender and Corporate Boards: The Route to a Seat at the Table*, Abingdon: Routledge.

Budig, M.J. and Hodges, M.J. (2010) Differences in disadvantage: variation in the motherhood penalty across white women's earnings distribution, *American Sociological Review*, 75(5): 705–728.

Cockburn, C. (1991) *In the Way of Women: Men's Resistance to Sex Equality in Organizations*, London: Macmillan.

Connell, R.W. (2020) *Masculinities*, Abingdon: Routledge.

Cummings, S., Bridgman, T. and Brown, K.G. (2016) Unfreezing change as three steps: rethinking Kurt Lewin's legacy for change management, *Human Relations*, 69(1): 33–60.

de Vries, J.A. (2015) Champions of gender equality: female and male executives as leaders of gender change, *Equality, Diversity and Inclusion: An International Journal*, 34(1): 21–36.

Denning, S. (2004) Telling tales, *Harvard Business Review*, 82: 122–129.

Dobbin, F. and Kalev, A. (2016) Why diversity programs fail, *Harvard Business Review,* 94(7).

Eagly, A.H. and Carli, L.L. (2007) Women and the labyrinth of leadership, *Harvard Business Review*, 85: 63–71.

Elliott, K. (2016) Caring masculinities: theorizing an emerging concept, *Men and Masculinities*, 19(3): 240–259.

Ferry, N. and Guthey, E. (2020) *There is no lean in for men*, Academy of Management Annual Meeting Proceedings, https://doi.org/10.5465/AMBPP.2020.79

Fine, C. (2010) *Delusions of Gender – The Real Science Behind Sex Differences*, London: Icon.

Fletcher, J.K. (1999) *Disappearing Acts: Gender, Power, and Relational Practice at Work*, Cambridge (Mass): MIT Press.

Fletcher, J.K. (2004) The paradox of postheroic leadership: an essay on gender, power, and transformational change, *The Leadership Quarterly*, 15: 647–661.

Gill, R., Kelan, E.K. and Scharff, C.M. (2017) A Postfeminist Sensibility at Work, *Gender, Work & Organization*, 24(3): 226–244.

Goffee, R. and Jones, G. (2006) *Why should Anyone be Led by You?* Boston (Mass): Harvard Business School Press.

Gratton, L., Kelan, E. and Walker, L. (2007) *Inspiring Women: Corporate Best Practice in Europe*, London: The Lehman Brothers Centre for Women in Business, London Business School.

Gratton, L., Kelan, E., Voigt, A., Walker, L. and Wolfram, H.-J. (2007) *Innovative Potential: Men and Women in Teams*, London: The Lehman Brothers Centre for Women in Business, London Business School.

Hekman, D.R., Johnson, S.K., Foo, M.D. and Yang, W. (2017) Does diversity-valuing behavior result in diminished performance ratings for non-white and female leaders? *Academy of Management Journal*, 60(2): 771–797.

Hills, F. (2020) Diversity is being invited to the party; inclusion is being asked to dance. Available Under https://www.thedrum.com/opinion/2020/09/23/diversity-being-invited-the-party-inclusion-being-asked-dance [retrieved 12 August 2022].

Hodges, M.J. and Budig, M.J. (2010) Who gets the daddy bonus? Organizational hegemonic masculinity and the impact of fatherhood on earnings, *Gender & Society*, 24(6): 717–745.

Humbert, A.L., Kelan, E.K. and van den Brink, M. (2019) The perils of gender beliefs for men leaders as change agents for gender equality, *European Management Review*, 16(4): 1143–1157.

Ibarra, H. (2015) The authenticity paradox, *Harvard Business Review*, 93: 52–59.

Ibarra, H., Carter, N.M. and Silva, C. (2010) Why men still get more promotions than women, *Harvard Business Review*, 88: 80–85.

Kalev, A., Dobbin, F. and Kelly, E. (2006) Best practices or best guesses? Assessing the efficacy of corporate affirmative action and diversity, *American Sociological Review*, 71(4): 589–617.

Kanter, R.M. (1977) *Men and Women of the Corporation*, New York (New York): Basic Books.

Kanter, R.M. (1984) *Change Masters*, New York (New York): Simon and Schuster.

Kelan, E.K. (2009a) *Performing Gender at Work*, Basingstoke: Palgrave.

Kelan, E.K. (2009b) Gender fatigue: the ideological dilemma of gender neutrality and discrimination in organizations, *Canadian Journal of Administrative Sciences*, 26(3): 197–210.

Kelan, E.K. (2014) From biological clocks to unspeakable inequalities: the intersectional positioning of young professionals, *British Journal of Management*, 25(4): 790–804.

Kelan, E.K. (2015) Linchpin – Men, Middle Managers and Gender Inclusive Leadership, British Academy and Cranfield School of Management. Available Under https://www.dropbox.com/s/2w39jg263ndo6mh/Linchpin.pdf?dl=0 [accessed 17 March 2023].

Kelan, E.K. (2018) Men doing and undoing gender at work: a review and research agenda, *International Journal of Management Reviews*, 20(2): 544–558.

Kelan, E.K. (2020) The inclusive leader, the smart strategist and the forced altruist: subject positions for men as gender equality partners, *European Management Review*, 17(3): 603–613.

Kelan, E.K. (2022) Men as middle managers doing and undoing gender in organizations, *European Management Review*, 19(2): 236–247.

Kelan, E.K. and Dunkley Jones, R. (2010) Gender and the MBA, *Academy of Management Learning & Education*, 9(1): 26–43.

Kelan, E.K. and Wratil, P. (2014) Winning Hearts and Minds - How CEOs talk about gender parity. KPMG and King's College London. Available Under https://www.dropbox.com/s/a7bagocvmnysa0k/Hearts%20and%20Minds.pdf?dl=0 [retrieved 17 March 2023].

Kelan, E.K. and Wratil, P. (2018) Post-heroic leadership, tempered radicalism and senior leaders as change agents for gender equality, *European Management Review*, 15(1): 5–18.

Kelland, J., Lewis, D. and Fisher, V. (2022) Viewed with suspicion, considered idle and mocked working caregiving fathers and fatherhood forfeits, *Gender, Work & Organization*, 29(5): 1578–1593.

Kirsch, A. (2022) Revolution from above? Female directors' equality-related actions in organizations, *Business & Society*, 61(3): 572–605.

Kirton, G., Robertson, M. and Avdelidou-Fischer, N. (2016) Valuing and value in diversity: the policy-implementation gap in an IT firm, *Human Resource Management Journal*, 26(3): 321–336.

Lash, S. (2002) Individualization in a non-linear mode, in U. Beck and E. Beck-Gernsheim (eds), *Individualization - Institutionalized Individualism and its Social and Political Consequences* (pp vii–xiii), London: Sage.

Lewin, K. (1947) Frontiers in group dynamics: concept, method and reality in social science: social equilibria and social change, *Human Relations*, 1: 5–47.

MacInnes, J. (1998) *The End of Masculinity*, Buckingham: Open University Press.

Main, B.G.M. and Gregory-Smith, I. (2018) Symbolic management and the glass cliff: evidence from the boardroom careers of female and male directors, *British Journal of Management*, 29(1): 136–155.

Martin, P.Y. (2001) 'Mobilizing masculinity': women's experiences of men at work, *Organization*, 8(4): 587–618.

Meyerson, D. and Scully, M.A. (1995) Tempered radicalism and the politics of ambivalence and change, *Organization Science*, 6(5): 585–600.

O'Neill, R. (2015) Whither critical masculinity studies? Notes on inclusive masculinity theory, postfeminism, and sexual politics, *Men and Masculinities*, 18: 100–120.

OED (2002) Oxford English Dictionary Available Under https://www.oed.com [retrieved 17 March 2023].

Orgad, S. and Gill, R. (2021) *Confidence Culture*, Durham (North Carolina): Duke University Press.

Organ, D.W. (1996) Leadership: the great man theory revisited, *Business Horizons*, 39(3): 1–4.

Palacios-Huerta, I. (2022) Competitiveness among Nandi female husbands, *Proceedings of the National Academy of Sciences*, 119(17): https://doi.org/10.1073/pnas.211 7454119

Paoletti, J.B. (2012) *Pink and Blue: Telling the Boys from the Girls in America*, Bloomington (Indiana): Indiana University Press.

Phillips, A. and Taylor, B. (1980) Sex and skill: towards a feminist economics, *Feminist Review*, 6: 79–88.

Roberson, Q.M. (2006) Disentangling the meanings of diversity and inclusion in organizations, *Group and Organization Management*, 31(2): 212–236.

Robertson, B.J. (2015) *Holacracy: The New Management System for a Rapidly Changing World*, New York (New York): Henry Holt and Company.

Ryan, M.K. and Haslam, S.A. (2005) The glass cliff: evidence that women are over-represented in precarious leadership positions, *British Journal of Management*, 16(2): 81–90.

Ryan, M.K., Haslam, S.A., Morgenroth, T., Rink, F., Stoker, J. and Peters, K. (2016) Getting on top of the glass cliff: reviewing a decade of evidence, explanations, and impact, *Leadership Quarterly*, 27(3): 446–455.

Schein, V.E. (2001) A global look at psychological barriers to women's progress in management, *Journal of Social Issues*, 57(4): 675–688.

Schein, V.E. and Davidson, M. J. (1993) 'Think manager - think male' – managerial sex typing among U.K. business students, *Management Development Review*, 6(3): 24–28.

Schwiter, K., Nentwich, J. and Keller, M. (2021) Male privilege revisited: how men in female-dominated occupations notice and actively reframe privilege, *Gender, Work & Organization*, 28(6): 2199–2215.

Sczesny, S. (2003) A closer look beneath the surface: various facets of the think-manager-think-male stereotype, *Sex Roles*, 49(2003): 353–363.

Sparrowe, R.T. (2005) Authentic leadership and the narrative self, *The Leadership Quarterly*, 16: 419–439.

Wajcman, J. (1998) *Managing Like a Man*, Oxford: Blackwell.

Weick, K.E. (1984) Small wins: redefining the scale of social problems, *American Psychologist*, 39(1): 40–49.

Williams, C.L. (1992) The glass escalator: hidden advantages for men in the 'female' professions, *Social Problems*, 39(3): 253–267.

INDEX

Note: References to endnotes show both the page number and the note number (231n3).